Four Religions of Asia

Four Religions of Asia

A PRIMER

by

Herbert Stroup

1817

HARPER & ROW, PUBLISHERS

NEW YORK, EVANSTON, AND LONDON

294

5

LIBRARY OF CONGRESS CATALOG CARD NUMBER: 68-17587

E—T

To my friends
Abraham S. Goodhartz
Walter H. Mais

I count myself in nothing else so happy
As in a soul remembering my good friends.
Shakespeare

CONTENTS

PREFACE

This brief and elementary book seeks to describe in relatively simple form the four religions of Asia which have had their source in India. It is intended for the reader who has little or no understanding of the descriptive features of these religions, or for the person with knowledge who wishes to review. The beginning chapter, also brief and elementary, seeks merely to survey some of the general considerations which are implicit in a discriminating approach to the nature of religion itself, and may be skipped by the reader who wishes only to review the religions themselves.

Bibliographies are provided at the end of each chapter, including references to the sacred scriptures of these four faiths, where suitably available. Valuable but out-of-print volumes, deeply critical studies, and other books of acknowledged scholarly competence, have in the main not been included. Contrariwise, an effort has been made to include readily available paperback books, so that the student who seeks more information may purchase an inexpensive volume or more than one.

At the beginning of each of the chapters on the religions a glossary is provided of the technical terms employed within the chapter, although each word is generally defined where it first occurs. Diacritical marks associated with the ancient languages of these four religions have not been provided, since the volume is aimed at a general reading public rather than mature scholars concerned with technical details.

The chart of the four religions at the beginning of the book seeks merely to be a simplified means of anticipating or reviewing.

All quotations from the Old and the New Testaments have been taken from the Revised Standard Version.

My thanks go to my daughter, Trudi Ann Stroup, for the preparation of the indexes.

Also, I am indebted to Dean Murray Horowitz, my colleague and friend, who suggested some years ago that he would like to see me write a book without footnotes. I have taken his advice.

The writer has been concerned with the religions of India for more than twenty-five years. He was a student of the subject under Robert E. Hume at Union Theological Seminary in New York City, where his degree thesis was on "The Conception of the Divine in the Upanishads." At that time he was also a student of Sanskrit in the Department of Indo-Iranian Languages of Columbia University under the late Anthony Paura and the late Louis Herbert Gray. Much later and under the auspices of Church World Service he had the occasion to visit India. In these ways and through reading on the subject, the writer formed a basis for composing this book.

Although indebted to many persons, including those mentioned above, he must remain responsible as do all authors for the substance of his work.

A COMPARISON OF FOUR RELIGIONS OF ASIA

Religion	Date of Founding	Founder	Title of Founder	Chief Scriptures	Main Divisions	Number of Adherents	Main Location
Hinduism	Prehistoric			Vedas Brahmanas Upanishads	Saivas Saktas Vishnavas	200–350 million	India, Pakistan, and elsewhere in Southeast Asia
Jainism	6th century B.C.	Vardhamana	Mahavira	Agamas	Shvetambaras Digambaras	1 to 1.5 million	India: Bombay, Central Provinces and Berar, Orissa Pakistan: Sind
Buddhism	6th century B.C.	Siddartha	Buddha	Tripitaka	Theravada Mahayana	150 million	Ceylon, Burma, Thailand, Viet Nam, China, Tibet, Korea, Japan, Mongolia
Sikhism	15th century A.D.	Nanak	Guru	Granth Sahib	Akalis Nanapanthis Udasis Khalsa Nirmalis Sewapanthis	6 million	India: Punjab, Central Provinces and Berar, Orissa Pakistan: Sind, Baluchistan

*Religions of Asia
and Elsewhere*

I

RELIGIONS OF ASIA
AND ELSEWHERE

INTRODUCTION

RELIGION IS A universal fact of human experience. At no time or place in human history has it been absent. Its forms may vary as external and internal forces play upon it. The forms, moreover, are manifested in all societies in special if not unique expressions. But man, both individually and collectively, apparently can no more escape being religious than he can deny the existence of the external world or eliminate his breathing. Man may be defined as the religious animal.

Such a view of the universality of religion is congenial to the Judeo-Christian tradition. The psalmist of the Old Testament, for example, says that "the heavens declare the glory of God: and the firmament showeth his handiwork." God's communication through

Similarly, in the Christian tradition, the writer of the Book of nature, the psalmist holds, is universal. Again, "There is no speech nor language, where their voice is not heard." The whole world is encompassed by the glory and handiwork of God: "Their line is gone out through all the earth, and their words to the end of the world." Hebrews began his exposition to the Jews of his time on the theme of the culmination of their hopes in Jesus as the Messiah by declaring the universality of God, who "at sundry times and in divers matters spake in time past unto the fathers by the prophets." And Jesus, although his meaning may have been quite restricted, is reported in the Gospel of John as saying · "Other sheep I have which are not of this fold."

3

The histories of both Judaism and Christianity provide ample evidence that they did not grow up like mushrooms in the dark. Rather, both religions were always part of a turbulent and threatening culture beyond themselves in which so-called pagan religions were vital challenges. Judaism and Christianity were well aware of the fact that they were not the only religions in the world. In this respect they were not unique; other religions, such as those of India and elsewhere, also possess an awareness of themselves in relation to other faiths.

Because of the universal and highly complex character of religion, it is appropriate that some introductory remarks be made about the nature of religion itself in order that the later study of four religions of Asia undertaken here (Hinduism, Jainism, Buddhism, and Sikhism) be properly oriented and hopefully better understood. For these religions, which originated in India, are—like Judaism and Christianity—merely some of the religions of mankind. They need to be approached from the standpoint of a basic understanding of the nature of religion itself and of its relationships to such other elements within culture as magic, morality, and science, to name only a few. This review and summary, however, is certainly not exhaustive and is not intended to do more than to provide some introductory information for elementary consideration.

METHODS OF CLASSIFYING RELIGIONS

Religions may be classified in a variety of ways. The four reviewed in this book are limited by their geographical source. The origin of each is confined to that area of Asia which, prior to 1947 (when the British withdrew as a colonial power), was known as India. In many respects the historical and cultural aspects of ancient India have survived to the present time, despite even the influence of colonialism.

Since the Second World War, India has split into two political entities. Although the religions with which we are concerned had their geographic origin in what are now India and Pakistan, all have not been confined to that region. Historically, Buddhism, which originated in India, spread beyond the borders of the land until it has become the most popular religion in Asia. On the other hand, Hinduism, Jainism, and Sikhism are almost exclusively to be found within India and Pakistan. Thus geographical origin is the primary delimiting factor for the present study, although the influence of these religions, direct and indirect, has been felt throughout the whole of Asia and, indeed, the world.

Admittedly, there are a number of other ways in which religions may be classified. First, they may be viewed chronologically—in terms of the date of their founding. In this context, Hinduism is possibly the oldest religion in the world. Scholars say that it may have been born as early as 2000 B.C. Sikhism is one of the youngest of religions. Usually, its origin is tied to the life of its founder, Nanak, whose birth date is 1469 A.D. Between these two points in time are found Buddhism, Christianity, Confucianism, Islam, Jainism, Judaism, Shintoism, Taoism, and Zoroastrianism.

Second, religions may be classified as living or dead. Those mentioned thus far are living religions. Many highly significant religions have come upon the world scene only to pass out of existence as the cultures in which they survived lost their vitality and disappeared. The religions of such ancient societies as Phoenicia, Babylonia, Egypt, Greece, Rome, Mexico, and Peru all bear testimony, along with others, to the fact that religions are not necessarily permanent in the world. The four religions of Asia discussed in this book, however, are still living religions.

Third, religions may be considered in terms of their aspiration to universality. There are only three that openly proclaim universal scope: Buddhism, Christianity, and Islam. Other religions, including three originating in India, seem to be hereditary or national systems.

NATURE OF RELIGION

The several ways of classifying religions, however, do not by themselves lead into the inner nature of religion itself. Answers to the question "What is religion?" must be found on other grounds. This question clearly implies that, despite great variety and complexity among the religions of the world, one can discover some common element or elements by which the phenomenon of religion might adequately be defined. The search for the fundamental nature of religion has engaged the best efforts of many scholars over the centuries. Unfortunately, there is no common agreement on the subject at present. A review of several definitions, however, may prove helpful.

The English word "religion" derives from the Latin *religio*. Even so, there is no clear agreement as to the meaning of the word. Servius and others, for example, held that it came from the root "lig-", which means "to bind." Religion in this sense would signify a relationship—the binding relationship between man and God. Yet Cicero believed that the word was derived from the root "leg-", which means "to take up, gather, count, or observe." The meaning here suggests the observation of the signs of divine communication. In later times, both meanings were accepted by Augustine, for example, and today there seems to be little if any question regarding the propriety of either derivation.

At times the deeper meaning of religion is not at all signified by the use of the word or by words related to it. Sometimes a form of the word is used as a substitute for "regularly," as in "He practices the piano religiously." At other times it signifies intensity of commitment or interest, as in "He is a religious student of opera." In such a case, "religious" is employed as a substitute for "earnest." Apparently no clear, final, or complete understanding of the nature of religion can be formulated etymologically.

A second way of defining the nature of religion is by the selection of a substantive element which undergirds universal religious experience. Historically, those who have used this method have sought to isolate a single factor which best represents and expresses its central meaning. It has been suggested, for example, that religion is primarily an intellectual activity. This view holds that religion is closely identified with theology and philosophy, and that it seeks to provide an intellectually coherent and defensible explanation of the totality of the created order. Another approach emphasizes the importance of the emotions. From this standpoint, religion is primarily a feeling. It may be a feeling of dependence upon the divine in all circumstances of life. It may involve positive emotional experiences such as joy and wonder, ecstatic experiences which are exceptional to ordinary living. Likewise, morality has been suggested as the single factor that reveals the nature of religion most profoundly; in other words, the core of religion consists of "commandments" or injunctions to ethical conduct. Again, the nature of religion has been defined as the implementation of the noblest social values held by a given society. In this view, religion possesses primarily a social function. It gives order and values to society deemed absolutely essential for the well-being of its citizens.

Several defects in each of these definitions, however, are immediately obvious. First, each is incomplete in itself. Taken singly, each stresses an important facet of religion, but hardly provides a comprehensive understanding of its nature. Second, each is relatively abstract and colorless. By reducing the enormous complexity of the various religions to a simple component, each tends to obscure the concrete forms in which religions are found in human history. *Homo religiosus* seemingly can never find adequate words to express completely what he means by being religious or having a religion.

A third approach to an understanding of the nature of religion stresses functional analysis. It seeks to avoid metaphysical debate, forgoing the cognitive quest for a factor or factors which fundamentally comprise religion. It admits that religions do exist and that they possess empirical features which are worthy of serious study. The primary interest of the functionalists, who are numerous today in the fields of anthropology and sociology, lies in the question "For what human ends are religions used?" Whether or not a religious belief or practice is true does not greatly concern these persons. They are chiefly interested in the manner in which religion satisfies certain individual and social needs.

Two examples may be helpful. First, a primary function of religion is that of maintaining the social order. Every social order requires the sanctification of various approved means and ends by which the well-being of the individual may be secured and maintained and the harmonious interrelationships of individuals within a society controlled. Second, religion has the function of sustaining the equilibrium of the individual. Life is filled with experiences which throw men into a state of unbalance or disequilibrium. They are born into a largely hostile environment. Throughout life they are threatened with the obliterating fact of death. Between life and death they are influenced by a variety of unsatisfying and frustrating experiences. Religion possesses the function of strengthening a man's ability to persist in his efforts to maintain his equilibrium. As such it is a compensatory feature of individual life, providing him with a powerful agency for understanding and overcoming those disabilities, both potential and actual, which otherwise would imperil, neutralize, or destroy him. These are some of the definitions of religion created by those who seek to understand its core meaning by analyzing what it does in human affairs.

A fourth way of defining the nature of religion emphasizes descriptive factors. The first method is linguistically oriented; it seeks to discover the meaning of religion through an analysis of words. The second depends highly upon logic and semantics; it has a tendency to define religion in terms of a single and basic element. The third seeks to relate the nature of religion to the satisfaction of human needs; its concern is limited to the function of religion. The fourth approach is clearly related to the other three, yet it defines religion somewhat differently. Religion seen from this perspective consists of the religions, one and severally, which have existed or which now exist. Such a view perceives religion as a particular social system existing within the larger framework of a group or a society. As a social system religion relates to other social systems within society, such as those of politics, education, economics, and the military. In fact, a society, aside from being a social system itself, consists of the interaction of a number of social systems or subsystems, of which religion is one. At some points the religious factor in a society may be clearly differentiated from others. But at other points it may be only indirectly identifiable as such. Religion and non-religion are a continuum in which it is often difficult to distinguish the separateness of any one element. There is, therefore, a valid meaning to the idea that religion is the institutionalized ethos of a society or of a group within the society.

To define a religion's essential nature as a social system does not deny its close interrelationship with the rest of society. It simply involves the description of beliefs and practices which are assumed and declared by the members of the society as being in their estimation possessed of a religious dimension. Such an approach does not need to explain the utility of all aspects of a given religion. In fact, it may assume that nonutilitarian factors not only exist but are cherished in religion as well as in other aspects of life. Such a view need not spend its energy by seeking to isolate some unique factor within a particular religious system or among all of them together. Again, its task is not settled by careful definition.

In the following chapters the four religions which have originated in India will be described as social systems. The founders, if any are known, will be indicated and their lives briefly sketched. Since these religions, like all others, can be understood only within their historical context, some attention will be given to their history. This will include mention of their leaders, geographic spread, schisms, and current trends. An effort will also be made to describe the character of the sacred scriptures which provide major resources in any effort to understand a religion. Finally, the teachings of each religion will be outlined with major stress upon doctrines pertaining to God, the person, and society. These various factors taken together comprise the social system of a religion.

Admittedly, the approach to four religions of Asia outlined above is based upon certain basic assumptions. These are clearly those of Western civilization, including the Judeo-Christian tradition, in which the concepts and perspectives have rich and varied meaning. They are not necessarily those which are found among Asians. For example, the idea of God, as we shall see in each of the succeeding chapters, is not equivalent to the idea in Judaism and Christianity. Nor, in fact, is it identical among the four religions, or for that matter, within any one of them. Yet no one can understand these religions without recourse to the idea of God. In addition, the approach to an understanding of a religion by way of its concept of God is especially meaningful to the Western student.

What is true for the incomparability of ideas of God in the several religions, moreover, is also true for all their other aspects. The reader must be aware that the following chapters have all the advantages and disadvantages of the process in reverse: a review of Christianity, for example—by an Indian, say, who is steeped in Indian culture and Hinduism.

The nature of religion is sometimes confused or contrasted with the nature of magic, morality, and science. A brief investigation of the relationships between these several characteristics will, it is hoped, increase the understanding of the nature of religion.

MAGIC AND RELIGION

Quite commonly those who are skeptical about the validity of the claims of religions say that all religion is basically magic. This assertion is based on the assumption that religion and magic are false, or that each represents a nonrational and, therefore, unreliable activity. Several serious students of primitive peoples have advanced the notion, however, that magic is a primitive science. They assume it is a device whereby man seeks to control nature by supernatural means. These anthropologists assume that primitive men are aware of certain "laws" by which they can manipulate nature. The use of such laws is analogous to the use by scientists of basic principles through which they can control and exploit nature. Magic in this context consists of a variety of practices, based upon a spiritual conception of man, society, and nature, which are available to the individual and can be used by him for his own and others' well-being or harm. The concepts of religion and magic, however, bear more careful consideration.

Religion and magic are both similar and dissimilar. They are closely related, if not identical, at a number of points. Several mutualities may profitably be indicated. First, both are concerned with mysterious, supernatural powers. Both are essentially nonempirical. The forces on which both depend cannot be touched or measured, although they are real to those who believe in them. Second, both are essentially transscientific. In fact, they generally do not seek to supplant science and its methods. They are deployed mainly in spheres of human activity to which science makes no definitive contribution. Also, unlike science, they do not depend upon a tight rational method, but upon nonphysical elements which it is assumed transcend the powers of nature and, therefore, of science. Third, both religion and magic involve a ritual system. At the core of the system is the symbolic. Symbolic objects point to a reality beyond themselves. The form of the symbol may be mundane, but the direction in which it is pointing is sacred. A ritual is rarely, if ever, created to be performed only once. Contrariwise, a ritual's virtue lies in the fact that it may be employed over and over again. In this sense it is a system, that is, a regular and dependable means for accomplishing particular goals.

Fourth, both religion and magic are similar in that the management of their ritual systems depends, with few exceptions, upon a special group of individuals, priests and magicians, who employ a special set of skills in carrying out their responsibilities. Commonly in societies, those who are responsible for the maintenance of religion or magic are set aside from ordinary pursuits by the society to perform their specialized and sacred functions. Yet mere separation from society is not enough. The isolated individual also must be skilled in his specialized activities. A ritual system which is maintained by persons of mediocre capacity or indifferent skills may by this reason alone not be efficacious. All these elements—and there are more—support the idea that religion and magic have much in common. But there is another side to the story.

Religion and magic, while admittedly related, may be viewed as dissimilar. Such a view, it was previously suggested, is held by those who look upon magic as a kind of prescience, as though both magic and science consisted in the application of certain pragmatically effective means for the attainment of a beneficent state of nature and human existence. Actually, however, science rests upon reason and experimentation and demonstrable facts. When the efforts of the scientist do not bring about the desired results, certain hypotheses are revised; new ideas and instrumentalities are employed to attain the goal. Magic, on the other hand, rests upon emotion and unquestioned belief. It is generally not amenable to serious or radical modification. If the methods of the magician are not beneficial it is assumed that some countermagic or some failure in the ritual system is responsible.

Also, as several anthropologists have shown, primitive peoples are not as naïve as they are assumed to be. They generally are capable of clearly distinguishing between magic and science. If the primitive person does not have a science, he surely has a technology. He is quite knowledgeable in his methods of securing shelter, hunting and gardening, child-rearing, and in creating effective means of transportation. Primitive man uses his technology for all it is worth. He has no thought of substituting magic for it; rather magic is a supplement to technology. Its usefulness is largely limited to those situations in which technology is inadequate, where ordinary human efforts are not able to conquer acknowledged evils. Of course, there are situations in which magic and technology are blended, since both should be conceived of as particular elements on a continuum of human experience.

If magic and science are somewhat different in their nature and function, so may religion and magic be. Several dissimilarities between them may be delineated briefly. First, magic is a nonmoral instrumentality. It may be used for both good and evil. It may be employed to benefit one's own well-being or to harm an enemy. Hence, there is black magic and white magic. Religion generally is moral in its intention. It very often seeks the good of all.

Second, religion and magic differ as to their goals. Magic is related to relatively concrete or specific goals. It operates in highly definable situations and is neither theologically nor philosophically astute. Religion, on the other hand, is more likely to be identified with broader and vaguer goals. These are apt to be more diffuse, and therefore not as readily managed by its ritual system. Magic is primarily manipulative, while religion is basically supplicative.

Third, magic seeks to achieve individual ends. It is more self-centered than religion. It seeks in a specific situation to employ a procedure for the benefit of one who has expressed a need. Magic is seldom employed to attain group ends. Religion, on the other hand, may be employed by individuals for their own benefit; yet it is regularly a shared experience within a group. Religion assumes that group benefits are to be sought as well as individual satisfactions. Magic contributes little to social cohesion, while religion, as many observers have noted, is a fundamental source of group solidarity.

Fourth, religion and magic differ on the subject of priest-layman or magician-client relationships. In magic both the practitioner and his client conduct the ritual system privately. The magician possesses a special talent. This talent and power is not related to the quality possessed by the group as a whole; it is his own possession. Again, the magician's client calls for a specific service to be performed for himself. The quality of the relationship between the magician and his client is not important. Also, magical acts are performed with a high degree of impersonality. They are efficacious for anyone for whom they are performed. Therefore, the client tends not to be fully involved in the ritual procedures.

Religion views the role of priest and layman in somewhat different terms. The priest has a different responsibility from that of the magician. He bears a responsibility for the believer, as he does for all believers within the group. The quality of personal relationship is relatively high. The priest believes himself to be a shepherd or prophet whose effectiveness is found, not in his own privately held powers, but in his ability to assist the believer in the attainment of private and social goals. Often the priest is not a private practitioner, but a representative of the group of which he is a part. A higher degree of emotion also characterizes religion. These dissimilarities—and there are others—indicate that religion, although closely related and even at times inextricably interwoven with magic, nevertheless differs from it. Each has a somewhat related but different function to perform.

Probably some sacred rites or ritual systems should be defined as magico-religious. That is, a complex rite often contains elements of both. For example, some specific element in the ritual system may be classified as magical, while the overall reverential awe, involving a sense of wonder and abasement in the presence of the sacred, may lead to the classification of the ceremony as essentially religious. Yet in other instances the two components may be readily separable.

MORALITY AND RELIGION

Religion and morality, like religion and magic, bear an ambiguous relationship to each other. This ambiguity is illustrated in part by the dispute in which some anthropologists have engaged as to which came first in human history. Some of these experts claim that religion is the earlier form. They even say that religion originally contained no moral elements and that its purpose was primarily to placate evil spirits who sought to do man harm. Others think that religion originally provided a moral code. The object of this code was to regulate personal and social behavior. The theological element, it is assumed, gave rise to the moral code. Later, the argument goes, men were more maturely able to acknowledge the implicit necessity for the moral code without knowledge of the religious base.

Yet equally competent anthropologists have claimed the opposite. They hold that a moral code was originally much more necessary to the maintenance of a group or society than any belief in supernatural powers. Moral relations derive intrinsically from human relations. Without morality society cannot exist. In fact morality is so important, they argue, to the continuance of a society, that supernatural sanctions tend to be applied to moral prescriptions in order to make them binding. In this view religion arose originally as a sanctification or projection of certain moral requirements held by groups or societies. The religious sanction added awe and reverence to what otherwise might be considered a human and even mundane social requirement.

Happily there is no need to choose between the two views. No one really knows how either religion or morality got started, since such matters have thus far been lost on the misty borders between prehistory and history. Nor is any exclusive benefit gained from either theory. Both acknowledge that for long periods of human history and in many differing societies religion and morality have had a closely interrelated existence. Again, it does not seem to be true, as some say, that a clear moral code is found only among the so-called advanced or sophisticated religions. A number of primitive religions give evidence of similar condition. For example, the Manus people of the Bismarck Archepelago possess an ethical religion. It employs supernatural powers as a direct support for a rather rigid code of morality. Religion and morality, then, cannot be separated in terms of either their origins or their intrinsic relationships, although they are not identical.

The relations between religion and morality can be described in three ways. Of these the first sees them as separate and quite unrelated. This view is supported in several ways. Some persons, convinced that the question of morality is an inferior one, assert that the prior need is the establishment of proper relations with God. They believe also that the quest for eternal salvation is so separate from moral issues and concomitantly so demanding as to require the major if not the sole effort of the believer. Any effort to combine religion and morality for these people tends to reduce the primacy of religion.

For others who likewise assert a radical chasm between religion and morality, religion is a matter of the supernatural and eternal order of things, while morality is concerned with the actual and changing configurations of human affairs. They may believe in both religion and morality, but they defend and practice them on different levels of logical acceptance. Thus in American society there are those who claim that religion has nothing to do with business or politics. To relate religion to either is to debase it and make it part of the creaturely world. To them religion and morality are quite separate. They would strongly and clearly differentiate between sin and badness. Sin is an evil action only in relation to divine standards. What is bad is defined as opposed to personal taste or social consensus.

A second view holds that religion and morality are closely related or even identical. For many Jews, for example, it would be difficult to argue that the Ten Commandments are a mere moral prescription. So, too, the Golden Rule for Christians. Many Jews and Christians would quickly aver that the person who does not accept and uphold the moral laws of the respective religions is not qualified to be looked upon as essentially either Jewish or Christian, since they believe these moral codes reflect the will of God. In fact, many would assert that the quality of a man's relationship to God is ascertained by observing the quality of his relations with his neighbors and his enemies.

In Western societies, however, where the Judeo-Christian tradition prevails, religion and morality have not always been viewed as intrinsically interrelated. Many Western Jews and Christians have been more concerned with moral matters than with abstract theology or the Church. This emphasis upon morality in contrast to religion, moreover, has been found periodically in the history of Christianity, as witness the monk Pelagius in the fifth century A.D. and the Anabaptists in Europe in the sixteenth. Such exceptions prove the rule. When they occur they often call forth prophets who seek to reestablish the interdependent relationships between religion and morality. Thus, much of the greatness of Søren Kierkegaard (1813-1855 A.D.) derives from his feeling that the churches in his time had become so preeminently concerned with morality that their essentially religious task was scarcely understood, appreciated, or given precedence.

Third, religion and morality may be viewed as separate but highly interrelated. From this standpoint the two bear a very complex relationship to each other. By no means can they be assumed to be identical, yet in their distinctiveness they lend support to each other. Caste in India, for example, is a cardinal feature of the social organization of that country; Hinduism is the predominant religion of the land. Caste and Hinduism are distinct social features, but despite their separateness they are closely interrelated.

The third view may be expressed in another way. Religion may be described as being focused primarily upon "is-ness," while morality is basically concerned with "ought-ness." Religion is an effort to penetrate the nature and meaning of reality at its depths. It seeks an understanding of the totality of human experience, embedded as it is in nature. Morality is more limited. It is concerned with the maintenance of the highest ethical standards. It senses the contrast, the continual falling away of what is from what ought to be. Its aim is limited to the interpersonal relationships of human beings.

Morality is concerned basically with human relations. It is possible to establish a morality without recourse to religion. Its substance is derived from the ordinary relationships of human beings as they come under the judgment of what might be. Religion, on the other hand, is also concerned with such relationships, but in addition possesses a cosmic outreach. Its concern with all aspects of behavior is rooted in suprasocial norms. Its field of interest covers not only man and man but also man and a higher power or powers.

SCIENCE AND RELIGION

An exploration of the relationship between religion and science may also contribute to an understanding of the nature of religion. The relations between religion and magic and between religion and morality are complex and at times confusing. But the relations between religion and science have perplexed many thoughtful minds even more, and have also touched off much vehement emotion in the course of their mutual development. It is almost impossible for any one to approach the subject of their interrelationships without some bias. Bias is part of every human expression; there is no such thing as complete objectivity. So it is within the limits of would-be impartiality that a description will be attempted.

There are, in fact, four clearly and widely held attitudes toward the interrelations of religion and science. These may be sketched briefly, recognizing that various combinations of the four are possible.

First, there is the view that only science provides sure knowledge. Those who hold this position sometimes assert that religion is the refuge of the ignorant. As knowledge increases, these say, there will be less and less need for religion. Religion is based not on fact, but on fancy. The decisive issues of human life are met in our times by scientific means.

Those who hold this opinion have much historical support. In the past, religion has been called upon to make many adjustments of its tenets. Some changes have been major ones, because scientific knowledge provided a more dependable understanding of man and his world. The history of the "warfare" of science with Christian theology demonstrates how effective science has been in forcing important modifications of the Christian world view. The successes of science have been so great that, whenever there is a conflict between religion and science, some will readily conclude that science is necessarily right. It may be true that religion also has had some impact upon the course of development of science; one may note, for example, that it has developed to its highest planes in dominantly Christian cultures. But the historical record is clear: Christianity, or what people assume to be Christianity, has regularly given way under the onslaught of science. The growth of science has largely led to the demystification of the world.

The view that only science provides sure knowledge has led some to predict that one day religion will be entirely eliminated by the growth of science. These advocates assume that the conflict between religion and science will continue, and that religion, because it is based on ignorance, will ultimately be forced to give way altogether. Indeed, the announced day for the total elimination of religion was placed by some as long as five decades ago; yet there seems to be no immediate prospect of its passing from the scene. In fact, science at certain times and places has been seized upon readily by religious persons and organizations as a benefit to their cause. It has been widely employed, for example, in the study of religion, particularly in understanding an element central to some of the religions: namely, their sacred scriptures.

Some claim that religion has persisted because it deals with realms where science can neither now nor in the future provide demonstrable knowledge. Three spheres commonly mentioned are: the nature of self; the nature of the world, including other selves; and the basis for values. Science may contribute to a richer and more accurate understanding of these realms of human concern, but—it is asserted—it will never be in a position to explain them satisfactorily. The self-transcending self may never be fully predicted and controlled by science. The knowledge provided by science regarding the world, including other selves, may always be partial and changing, despite man's need for a coherent interpretation of the totality of the self-existent. Again, science may never be able to provide a sure basis on which decisions involving preference or worth are made.

At any rate, no matter how valuable science may be now or in the future, there seems to be no justification for not knowing as much as possible about religion, since it obviously, and currently, plays a highly significant part in the lives of countless numbers of people throughout the world.

Second, others believe that no basic conflict exists between religion and science, each being quite independent or distinct. Those who take this position commonly say that religion and science involve two different methods of knowing reality, which they assume possesses a basic unity. Religion and science, therefore, are incomplete if taken separately. Together, they contribute to the fullest understanding of man, society, and nature. This argument obviously involves a parallelism. The method of science is reason, which, it is claimed, is readily adaptable to the observable, external, or objective world. Religion, on the other hand, employs the methods of faith. It seeks to relate the essentially subjective or inner-based experience of the individual with those nonempirical features of the world that have traditionally been termed spiritual. Thus reason and faith are used by man in parallel fashion to increase his understanding. From this angle, authentic conflicts between religion and science can hardly be said to exist. Skirmishes between the two do take place, it is admitted, but these are good; they reflect the tension between them (a result of the overall claims of religion and science), and the tension acts as a clarifier for method. Part of the problem of this view, however, is that it does not contain the resources within itself of explaining how the two methods can ultimately create a uniformly harmonious interpretation of human experience. Also, in a given circumstance, little or no guidance is provided as to which method can be regarded as more reliable.

Third, still others believe that religion, being a higher truth, is superior to science. Those who hold this position are somewhat in agreement with the parallelism of reason and faith described above, but they add the notion that the method of faith is generally, if not always, superior to that of reason. This view is somewhat the opposite of the first in this series.

One way of expressing the third position is to say that science is limited to the sphere of empirical causation, while religion is involved with the nature of meaning. Science is essentially descriptive. It seeks to describe the chain of relationships by which the objective world is known. But religion, utilizing the findings of science, is responsible for an additional and even superior contribution—that of adding meaning to what is known. Religion, it is said, is basically open to all empirically founded knowledge. It, too, desires an impartial accounting of all events. But once this is secured, religion then takes up the task of making sense of it. What do the disparate findings of science really mean? Also, how shall the conflicting contributions of science be effectively harmonized? By what principle shall "sure knowledge" be judged? What are the source and meaning of the presuppositions employed by science to secure its knowledge? These and other questions of meaning, it is claimed, relate science to a sphere which is nonscientific, and is ultimately the province of religion.

Religion, moreover, has the responsibility not merely of assigning meaning to scientific discoveries, but of formulating the basic values upon which human beings take action in relation to the findings of science. This responsibility places religion at the core of decision-making. Science may contribute to the task, but it must bow before the higher truth of religion.

Fourth, there are yet others who believe that religion and science are essentially harmonious in their relations or even identical. From this standpoint there is no need to assign superior-inferior positions to religion and science. Each is as worthy as the other. Religion will never take the place of science, nor is it a superior truth by which science itself is bound. Similarly, science will never displace religion. There is no need for that, since the interests and the methods of both are harmonious. Religion has both opposed and furthered science; so, too, science has both opposed religion and furthered it. They are like a man's two legs: each moving in harmony with the other enables him to progress. They are much alike, although at a single moment in time one may be ahead of the other.

The dilemma of reason vs. faith is assumed in this outlook to be a false choice. Rather, reason and faith together are said to be methods of both religion and science. A religion which rests entirely upon faith and makes no place for reason is intellectually shallow and unworthy of human attention. Theology, as well as other efforts in religion, attests to the high value religion assigns to reason, which has a corrective function to play in relation to faith.

As religion has need for reason, so science has need of faith. Sheer facts are in themselves inconceivable. Men are in motion so far as the development of knowledge is concerned, and this necessarily involves both them and their sciences in decisions for which no sure knowledge is available. The scientist who did not act by faith would never discover anything new. Like his counterpart in religion, he relies heavily upon a variety of methods.

Thus religion and science are not opposed, nor is one superior to the other. Viewed properly, it is said, they are in harmonious relation or even identical.

POSTSCRIPT

Earlier in this chapter the organization of succeeding chapters was briefly outlined. This constituted a statement of positive purpose. At the present point, however, let me say what this book is not. Such a negative declaration may provide an additional basis for understanding both the scope and the limits of the following chapters.

First, this book is in no sense a complete or exhaustive study of the subject. It is a primer. Clear dangers derive from oversimplification, and these are recognized so far as is humanly possible. The annotated bibliographies at the ends of the chapters and at the close of the book are meant to aid readers in the extension of their knowledge regarding these four religions of Asia. No documentation, moreover, has been included in this volume, and this is deliberate. The reader who is beginning or merely reviewing his knowledge of these four religions will not wish to be involved in the extensive complications that leading scholars see in them.

Second, this is not a study in comparative religion. Little effort will be made to compare the four faiths concerned. Such an aim is indeed worthy, but is not the one chosen here. The reader will readily be able to make comparisons of a variety of religious themes. He should make these on his own. The primary effort is not one of comparison, but of the descriptive elucidation of the essentials of each religion.

Third, no effort will be made to defend the Judeo-Christian tradition or any part of it. Actually, of course, the book has no direct relation with this tradition. There are books of merit which in all ages as well as this one have attempted to accomplish that purpose, but such responsibility has not been assumed in the writing of this book.

Fourth, no effort will be made to demean, criticize, or point up weaknesses in the religions of Asia, and no effort will be made to justify any aspect of them. In this spirit—that of earnest and scrupulous concern for the objective nature of these four religions, descriptively portrayed—the succeeding chapters have been formulated.

Fifth, the primary intention of this book is not to interpret the meaning and value of these four religions. Rather, it is simply to provide information, factual information, regarding them. The task of evaluation of a religion is legitimate and indeed desirable, but it has not been chosen for this effort. Before proper interpretation can be made, moreover, the evaluator must be thoroughly familiar with the descriptive features of a religion.

In the following pages, Hinduism and Buddhism are given more extensive treatment than Jainism and Sikhism. Both Hinduism and Buddhism have attracted many more adherents and are in many ways more complex social systems. Yet the comparatively extensive accounts of Jainism and Sikhism are based not on quantitative considerations, such as the number of adherents, but upon the fact that they, too, are religions which possess all the basic features and characteristics that are present in Hinduism and Buddhism.

ANNOTATED BIBLIOGRAPHY
ON FOUR RELIGIONS OF ASIA
AND ELSEWHERE

1 ANSHEN, RUTH. *Moral Principles of Action: Man's Ethical Imperative.* New York: Harper & Row, 1952. A discussion of the basic nature of ethics.

2 BAILLIE, JOHN. *Natural Science and the Spiritual Life.* New York: Oxford University Press, 1951. A theologian views the relations between science and religion.

3 BLANSHARD, BRAND. *Reason and Goodness.* New York: The Macmillan Co., 1961. A philosopher discusses the character of the ethical life.

4 BOUISSON, MAURICE. *Magic: Its History and Principal Rites.* New York: E. P. Dutton & Co., 1960. A sound and popular version of the nature of magic.

*5 BOUQUET, ALAN. *Comparative Religion: A Short Outline,* 5th ed. Baltimore: Penguin Books, 1956. A survey and comparison of the great religions of the world, but with little stress upon Jainism and Sikhism.

*6 ELIADE, MIRCEA. *The Sacred and the Profane: The Nature of Religion.* Translated by WILLARD R. TRASK. New York: Harper Torchbooks, 1961. Reflections on the nature of religion.

7 GARNETT, ARTHUR. *The Moral Nature of Man and Critical Evaluation of Ethical Principles.* New York: Ronald Press, 1952. A textbook on ethics.

*8 HALL, ALFRED. *The Scientific Revolution, 1500-1800: The Formation of the Modern Scientific Attitude.* Boston: Beacon Press, 1960. An historical interpretation of the rise of science.

9 KEETON, MORRIS. *Values Men Live By: An Invitation to Religious Inquiry.* New York: Abingdon Press, 1960. An introduction to the subject of religion.

10 LUNN, ARNOLD. *The Revolt Against Reason.* New York:
* Paperback.

Sheed & Ward, 1951. Shows the tendency in a scientific age to misunderstand and misuse reason.

*11   MALINOWSKI, BRONISLAW. *Magic, Science and Religion and Other Essays.* Garden City, N. Y.: Doubleday Anchor Books, 1948. A review of the historical contributions to the subject and some positive proposals.

12   NEILL, STEPHEN. *Christian Faith and Other Faiths.* New York: Oxford University Press, 1961. An attempt to understand non-Christian religions from a Christian standpoint.

13   PERRY, WILLIAM. *The Origin of Magic and Religion.* London: Methuen & Co., 1923. A careful review of the subject.

*14   PIGGOTT, STUART. *Prehistoric India.* Baltimore: Penguin Books, 1950. Presents the archeology of ancient India.

*15   SMART, HINIAN. *World Religions: A Dialogue.* Baltimore: Pelican Books, 1966. A novel approach through dialogue to the world's religions.

*16   TOULMIN, STEPHEN. *The Philosophy of Science.* New York: Harper Torchbooks, 1960. A comprehensive perspective on the foundations of science.

17   VETTER, GEORGE. *Magic and Religion: Their Psychological Nature, Origin and Function.* New York: Philosophical Library, 1958. A general account of the interrelations of magic and religion.

18   VIVAS, ELISEO. *The Moral Life and the Ethical Life.* Chicago: University of Chicago Press, 1950. An astute analysis of the nature of ethics.

*19   WACH, JOACHIM. *Sociology of Religion.* Chicago: Phoenix Books, University of Chicago Press, 1944. A scholarly analysis for advanced students.

*20   ——. *The Comparative Study of Religions,* ed. with an Introduction by JOSEPH M. KITAGAWA. New York: Columbia University Press, 1958. A technical and profound exploration of the nature of religious experience.

*21   WALLBANK, T. WALTER. *A Short History of India and Pakistan.* New York: Mentor Books, New American Library, 1958. A history of India from ancient times to the present.

22   WIDGERY, ALBAN. *What is Religion?* New York: Harper & Brothers, 1953. A review of the question by a philosopher.

23   YINGER, J. MILTON. *Religion, Society and the Individual: An Introduction to the Sociology of Religion.* New York: The Mac-

millan Co., 1957. A textbook on the sociology of religion, from the functional viewpoint, with a careful selection of readings from original sources.

*24 ZAEHNER, ROBERT, *The Comparison of Religions.* Boston: Beacon Press, 1962. A learned volume on the relations of non-Christian religions, especially Hinduism and Buddhism, to Christianity.

*25 ZIMMER, HEINRICH, *Philosophies of India,* edited by JOSEPH CAMPBELL, New York: Meridian Books, 1956. A long, philosophical account of Indian concepts and movements.

Hinduism

Einleitung

A GLOSSARY OF HINDU TERMS*

Advaita	Nondualistic philosophy expounded by Sankara.
Agamas	The scriptures of the Hindu sects, sometimes called *Tantras*.
Ahimsa	Noninjury, nonviolence, reverence for life.
Akasa	Ether.
Anumana	Inference.
Aryas	A population which considered itself to be of noble birth and descent.
Asrama	A hermitage.
Asramadharma	The four stages of life for the devout Hindu.
Atharvaveda	One of the Vedas.
Atman	The self.
Avatar	An incarnation.
Avidya	Ignorance.
Bhagavad Gita	A devotional classic, a part of the Mahabharata.
Bhakti	Devotion; also a social movement within Hinduism.
Brahmacharya	The stage in life of the student.
Brahmanas	Sacred scriptures of Hinduism devoted to ritualized religion.
Brahmans	Members of the priestly or intellectual caste.
Buddhi	Intellect.
Darsanas	The six schools of thought in Hinduism; also the literature of the schools.
Dasa	Those termed by the Aryans as inferior, the darker-skinned indigenous people of India, Dravidians.
Dharma	A duty or social obliagtion, a law, an essential quality, or any reality, right action.
Dharma Sastras	Codes of laws, manuals, digests, a part of the sacred scriptures of Hinduism.

* The same term may have a somewhat different meaning in the four religions.

29

Din-i-Ilahi	A syncretistic religion founded by Akbar in the sixteenth century A.D.
Dvaita	Dualistic philosophy taught by Ramanuja and Madhva.
Garhasthya	The stage in life of the householder.
Jati	Caste.
Jiva	The soul.
Jivan-mukta	The fully realized or liberated person.
Jivanmukti	A form of religious experience in which the Divine Life permeates the everyday life of believers.
Jnana	Saving knowledge.
Karma	The principle of causality in moral experience.
Kshatriyas	Members of the warrior or ruling caste.
Linga	A phallus, a symbol of Siva.
Mahabharata	An epic, a part of the sacred scriptures of Hinduism.
Mahat	Great or worthy.
Mimamsa	An orthodox school of Hindu thought, based on an investigation of the Vedas.
Moksha	Ultimate release or salvation.
Nibandhas	Writings on family and religious subjects, a part of the sacred scriptures of Hinduism.
Nyaya	An orthodox school of Hindu thought, based on logical realism.
Pandit	A teacher.
Prakriti	Objective existence.
Pranayama	Breath control, a *yoga* technique.
Pratyakasha	Perception.
Puranas	Pious legends about deities and heroes, a part of the sacred scriptures of Hinduism.
Purusha	The nonmaterial elements of the universe.
Ramayana	An epic, a part of the sacred scriptures of Hinduism.
Rigveda	One of the Vedas.
Rita	The order of natural events and at times the moral order.
Sabda	Credible testimony.
Saivism	A Hindu sect which worship the god Siva.

Saktism	A Hindu sect which worships the female god Sakti.
Samaveda	One of the Vedas.
Samkhya	An orthodox school of Hindu thought, based on evolutionary dualism.
Samsara	The world of phenomenal existence.
Sannyasa	The stage in life of the ascetic.
Sati	The practice of widow-burning, sometimes called suttee.
Smriti	The auxiliary literature of Hinduism.
Sruti	Revealed teachings in Hinduism.
Sudras	Members of the agricultural and artisan caste.
Sutras	Manuals of ritualism, a part of the sacred scriptures of Hinduism.
Tantras	The scriptures of the Hindu sects, sometimes called *Agamas*.
Upamana	Analogy.
Upanishads	Contemplative scriptures of Hinduism.
Vaiseshika	An orthodox school of Hindu thought, based on realistic pluralism.
Vaishnavism	A Hindu sect which worships the god Vishnu.
Vaisyas	Members of the commercial and agricultural caste.
Vanaprasthya	The stage in life of the hermit or recluse.
Varna	Sanskrit name for caste, meaning "color."
Varnadharma	The caste system.
Vedangas	Practical writings, a part of the sacred scriptures of Hinduism.
Vedanta	An orthodox school of Hindu thought, based on an extension of Vedic concepts.
Vedas	The earliest scriptures of Hinduism.
Yajurveda	One of the Vedas.
Yoga	An orthodox school of Hindu thought, based on disciplined meditation; also the method and practice leading to union of the self with the divine.

II

HINDUISM

INTRODUCTION

THE COMPLEX RELIGION known as Hinduism is the world's oldest living religion. Its origins are clouded by the misty beginnings of Indian history. Some scholars put the date of its birth as early as 2000 B.C., but most agree that the historical period of India, and therefore of Hinduism, begins with the invasion of Aryan tribes somewhere between 1500 and 1200 B.C. While Shintoism, the immemorial religion of Japan, and Judaism are also quite ancient, they probably cannot compete with Hinduism in age.

Hinduism is one of the world's largest living religions. The dozen or so religions still ritually practiced in the world have attracted a widely differing number of adherents. Some apparently appeal to relatively few people; such are Zoroastrianism with about 100,000 followers and Jainism with about 1.5 million. On the other hand, a number of the living religions of the world continue to attract many millions of people. Absolutely accurate statistics on such matters admittedly are not available, but it is possible to say that some of the largest living religions are Buddhism, Christianity, Confucianism, Hinduism, and Islam. Hinduism is surely noteworthy for its large number of adherents. Some serious students of the subject maintain that the number ranges from 200 to 250 million; other equally competent authorities say that the followers of Hinduism range between 300 and 350 million. Actually no one knows the exact number. What is certain is that Hinduism possesses wide appeal.

Hinduism is further notable because it has mothered more religions than any other contemporary faith. Most existing religions have

32

been content to be themselves. Some have claimed to be final and conclusive; they are therefore not prone to give birth to new faiths. A notable exception is Judaism, which forms the basis for two other living religions: Christianity and Islam. Hinduism, however, has given birth to three religions which today are potent influences in the lives of their followers: Jainism, Buddhism, and Sikhism. Each of these, described separately in later chapters, owes its historical and cultural point of origin to Hinduism.

While these four religions of Asia will be treated separately in this book, the reader should bear in mind that they possess a close relationship to each other. They are bound together, it is true, by a common geographic base. But more importantly, they all have grown up in a single though complex culture. They are like a tree. The common root system is Indian culture. The trunk of the tree, religiously speaking, is Hinduism. The tree also has branches: these are Buddhism, Jainism, and Sikhism. The tree is a whole; the branches take on meaning as a result of their connection with the trunk and its root system. Tree, trunk, and branches may be studied separately, but their relations are basic. Hinduism achieved a fundamental understanding of reality and life; the three other religions are linked to it.

Hinduism is distinctive, moreover, in being so largely confined to one geographic area: namely, India and Pakistan. Shintoism seems to be distinctive in the same way, since it has been confined to Japan. One might think that Judaism also fits this category, yet careful thought will indicate that it is the religion of a people who are not geographically confined, but have spread actually into many parts of the world. Certain other religions, such as Jainism in modern India and Pakistan, and Taoism in China, are found almost wholly within national borders. But these differ from Hinduism in that they do not constitute the faith of the vast majority within their geographic or national boundaries. Hinduism is the major religion, historically and currently, of the people of India, as well as a good-sized minority in Pakistan.

Although Hinduism is the religion of a particular people, its influence has spread to a great part of Asia as well. Several factors account for this: trade, political conquests, and the emigration of Indian colonists to various parts of Asia. Archeological findings also affirm the direct and indirect influence of Hinduism outside India in literature, sculpture, architecture, and language, as well as in religion itself. In fact, so far as Hinduism is concerned, traces of this religion are to be found wherever Buddhism took root in Asia.

There are chiefly three living religions which have claimed universality in scope and have sought to achieve such status through missionary zeal. These are: Buddhism, Christianity, and Islam. Each has claimed to be potentially the religion for everyone—without national, racial, geographic, or cultural distinction—and each is presently found in many parts of the world. Each has carried out its mission to a remarkable degree. Hinduism, on the other hand, has never claimed to be universal in the same sense. Its generous and tolerant views might have provided it with an appeal far beyond the borders of the old India, but Hinduism has never seen fit to develop an international missionary movement. The fact is that it has been relatively content to be the religion of the Indian people. The close relationship of Hinduism to the social order in India historically—its inextricable relationship to the caste system—also has limited its possibilities for universalization.

Today it is widely recognized in India and elsewhere that Hinduism is undergoing a resurgence. In part its renewal is the result of enormous political and social changes introduced within recent years. Following the withdrawal of Great Britain from India in 1947 and the partitioning of the land into India and Pakistan, Hinduism has been faced with the need to grapple once more with its essential nature. India, for example, seeks in its independence to be democratic. Its conception of democracy must be related to India's past, the nature of its people, and their present needs. Indian society in the past, based as it was on the caste system, can hardly be said to be democratic as most Western nations define democracy. In the face of this new democratic thrust, therefore, the followers of Hinduism have had to rethink its fundamental relationship to Indian society. This process continues.

Similarly since the partition of India in 1947, the question has arisen of the formal relationship between religion and the state. The government of India is avowedly a secular government. It has not declared Hinduism to be the state religion. Yet historically Hinduism has been most pervasive in all aspects of Indian life. Advocates of the religion are now faced with the problem of conceiving and defining Hinduism in such a way as to take the new political situation properly into account.

In this connection it is interesting to note that the dedicated and fiercely nationalist Jan Sangh or All-India People's party is today quite active. It strongly advocates the nation's traditions, holding that the nation should become once more a religious state, a Hindu state. The Jan Sangh is the political spearhead of a larger movement which is the Hindu Resurgence Movement.

In addition to the stimulus of democracy and secularism, Hinduism, as is true with any great religion, has itself been constantly in a state of change. Its own history, the variety of its expressions, the impact of religious and nonreligious ideas from beyond India, and other factors have spurred its continuing task of reassessment. Thus today, by reason of influences from without and from within, Hinduism is undergoing broad and deep renewal.

FOUNDER

Hinduism cannot point to any person in its history as its founder. It is primarily an ethnic expression. It grew up gradually over a period of about four thousand years, taking into itself all manner of religious and cultural movements in India. Only one other current religion, Shintoism, is without a personal founder.

In all other religions, with the possible exception of Judaism, there are fairly dependable accounts of the manner in which the religion was established by a person. In the case of Judaism, Moses is commonly considered to be the founder of the religion. Some persons may consider Abraham as being in truth the founder of Judaism, but it seems clear that Judaism as a fairly systematic and continuous heritage began with Moses. Interestingly, all religions which have personal founders revere a man, not a woman.

Some of the world's living religions not only have a personal founder but also a small group of loyal disciples who during his lifetime and after his death have played a major role in securing the place of the religion in human history. One thinks immediately, for example, of Jesus and his disciples. But Hinduism is distinctive in that no such band appears at the point of its origin. The Aryan invaders of antiquity can hardly fill the bill.

The lack in Hinduism of a personal founder and of an original group of advocates has influenced the character of the religion until the present time. The personal founder of a religion enjoys the opportunity, by reason of his authority, of defining its essentials precisely. He also has the possibility of exemplifying in his own life, often in heroic proportions, the exact nature of the religious expression to which he is committed. Usually one sees the nature of a religion in the personal life of its founder more clearly than anywhere else.

Hinduism is what it is to a marked degree because of its lack of such a personal element. There is no one in the past to which the follower can point as embodying the full human meaning of the religion. Nowhere in time does it become decisively personalized.

Yet a complex social system such as Hinduism did have a beginning, and this obviously involved persons. The Vedas, for example, are assigned to names, they contain specific references to natural phenomena and show a development in understanding and practice. These earliest scriptures of Hinduism indicate that Hinduism surely had a beginning, and that the beginning is expressed in a tradition. Hinduism was founded by persons who reacted to the world and who created common responses. Yet these persons are not the equivalent of a single, personal founder who epitomizes a religion in his life and teachings.

Seen in one perspective, Hinduism is a single religion; from another viewpoint it is many. Scarcely any thread, unless it be that of caste, runs through the totality of the faith. It combines religious beliefs and forms, as will be seen later, in such loose and diverse fashion as to create a serious question regarding its unity. Although Jainism, Buddhism, and Sikhism—to which Hinduism gave birth—are today separate religions, specific traces of them exist within Hinduism. Even elements of Christianity and Judaism may be found in it.

In addition to the important contributions of the Aryan invaders there are influences imbedded in Hinduism from the preinvasion period. Most of the major philosophical, theological, cultural, ritualistic, artistic, and other innovations in India's long life may also be found in one form or another within this faith. Hinduism is not like a building planned by an architect and created in exact detail to specifications. Rather it is like a river making its way from small and distant beginnings, meandering in its course as it finds the channels that will carry its flow, until by the time it reaches the open sea it has become so extensive as to seem unrelated to its distant source.

Hinduism as a consequence has possessed an enormous charity toward all ideas and movements not a part of itself. It is not a fanatical faith with an inflexible creed. It does not constantly vaunt itself as the one and only religious truth. Several types of religion, found elsewhere as clearly independent expressions, exist harmoniously within Hinduism. There is no agency within the religion to ferret out heretics. Few religious conflicts have existed among Hinduism's adherents historically; mainly, Hindus have been highly tolerant of each other. This traditional diversity and tolerance have resulted also in a lack of proselytizing activities as well.

Yet Hinduism and its history have not been without some conflict and even violence. The partition of British India released the murderous antagonisms which existed between Hindus and Muslims. Also, sudden violence has taken place on a sporadic basis upon the rumor of the killing of a sacred cow. But, despite these events, Hinduism has been notably easygoing and tolerant.

HISTORY

Since Hinduism is the oldest living religion of the world, its history is obviously detailed and complex. This description of it is not aimed at exhaustive recapitulation of its multifarious elements, but rather seeks to provide its major features in skeletal form.

The history of Hinduism does not follow precisely the chronology of the history of India. Students of that country's political life usually speak of three periods: first, the Hindu, extending from approximately 2000 B.C. to about 1200 A.D.; second, the Islamic conquerors, who dominated until about 1750 A.D., although there were many places in India where their rule was not operative; and third, the period of British rule, which lasted only about a century and a half, that is, from about 1800 to 1947 A.D. Hinduism of course, through all the centuries of changing circumstances of political rule in India, has been the religion of the masses. In that sense the recounting of the political history of India does not do full justice to the complex development of the religion itself.

Hinduism was initially the creation of a society which predates the Aryan invasion of India. Archeological findings, beginning in 1922 in the Punjab and the Indus valley, show that a highly developed urban culture was in existence between 3000 and 2000 B.C. in the ancient cities of Harappa,—prehistoric capital of the Punjab, situated on the left bank of the river Ravi—and Mohenjodara (Mound of the Dead) on the right bank of the Indus, four hundred miles to the southwest in Sind. These two cities, like the contemporary settlements of Mesopotamia and Egypt, were related to the great rivers and the broad fertile plains of the region. The excavators found considerable support in the Indus valley civilization for a number of historical features of Hinduism. For example, they discovered the remains of a place where ceremonial ablutions probably were performed as they are in Hindu temples now. Apparently it was the responsibility of the priests of that day to perform ablutions at an appointed time and to officiate at public gatherings held there on notable ceremonial occasions. Water as a symbol of purification in Hinduism may well have had its origins then. Other anthropological findings also tend to support the theory that Hinduism is derived from this pre-Aryan culture: the worship of the Mother-goddess, figures seated on a stool as in the position of a yogi in meditation, prototypes of the Indian god Siva as the Lord of the Beasts, and symbols of the male and female generative organs.

This view of the two ancient cities, however, is challenged by other scholars. Some authorities say they were originally related to Sumerian civilization, and that either the citizens lost their vital hold on life and drifted into disintegration or the cities themselves were overrun by the Aryans when they entered the area.

About 1500 B.C., at any rate, quite a different religious tradition was introduced into the deserted and ruined Indus cities. At that time the Aryans, people of Indo-European stock and language, tall and light-skinned, flowed through the passes of the Hindu Kush mountains into northwest India, where they found the earlier cities in ruin, probably destroyed by barbarians from the West. The impact of the vigorous Aryans upon the bearers of the Indus civilization gave an enormous stimulus to the creative faculties of all, resulting in the higher developments in religion which later characterized Hinduism.

The term "Aryan" actually signifies a linguistic grouping like "Semitic." Yet it also represents a group of people who, about 1500 B.C., migrated from the region between southern Russia and Turkestan. One segment of the group carried their language, Sanskrit, to the west, where they found counterparts in Europe who comprised the *centum* linguistic group, including Latin, Greek, Celtic, Teutonic, and the Germanic and Slavonic languages. Those who proceeded eastward introduced Sanskrit and the whole complex of the Aryan civilization into India. Originally they settled in the small villages of the Punjab with their flocks and herds; later they permeated the whole of India. The Aryans believed themselves to be of noble birth and descent. That is the meaning of *aryas*. They contrasted themselves with the darker-skinned inhabitants remaining in the Indus valley. These they called *dasa,* a term of reproach which later came to mean "slave" in Sanskrit. The word "Dravidian" is the modern counterpart of *dasa.* As the Aryans met and conquered the indigenous peoples of India, they found it appropriate and even necessary to organize the resulting society on an intellectually defensible basis. Early Hinduism in part reflects the century-long effort of the Aryans to make sense of their relationships to other peoples. Socially the caste system, which will be described later, became the eventual means of creating and sustaining social harmony between the two groups in a religiously supported fashion. The results of the events of this early period, religiously, socially, and in other ways, remain a part of Hinduism to the present day.

The historical span of time which approximately covers the events just outlined is designated as the Vedic period. Its beginning and end are difficult to place precisely in the chronology of Hinduism. Possibly it began as early as 2000 B.C. Probably it does not extend later than 500 B.C., since its literature (from the Vedas to the chief Upanishads) predates the life of Buddha, who died about 483.

The events of the period, especially those of religious importance, are embodied in three successive stages of literature: The Vedas, the Brahmanas, and the Upanishads.

The Vedas portray those efforts in early Hinduism by which the personified forces of nature, such as fire, wind, and rain, were recognized, philosophized about, and traced under the concept of cosmic order (rita) as the supreme law over both gods and men. In the early literature the gods are many. They are not clearly differentiated; sometimes the same name is ascribed to more than one deity and the same power attributed to a number of them. In time, however, two of the gods were recognized as predominant: Indra, the god of power, and Varuna, the god of righteousness. Even later a series of supreme deities was acknowledged: Prajapati or Lord of Creatures, Aditi or the Infinite, Prana or Life, and Kala or Time. Rita or cosmic order remained as perhaps the most important idea of the period. Originally rita signified the order of natural events, such as the regular succession of the seasons and the movement of celestial bodies. But later the moral as well as the natural order fell within its meaning.

The Brahmanas are primarily treatises on sacrificial rites. They emphasize ritualized religion. This kind of religion was based upon prior developments. Since under the notion of rita the gods were thought to be in control of both the moral and the natural order, it was thought that they had to be propitiated by means of sacrifice. In time sacrifice grew in importance as the primary device for the harmonious maintenance of people's lives. The rituals were defined and elaborated extensively in the Brahmanas.

In the Brahmanic period, moreover, the priesthood rose to social preeminence. The sacrifical ceremonies were of primary importance, and they depended for their faithful and correct conduct upon a professional class of priests. Probably in this period the doctrines of caste and the four stages of life, discussed below, were formulated, putting the priests in the top position.

The Upanishads represent a contemplative trend in Hinduism which grew up in part as a response to the excesses of the priestly and sacrificial period that preceded them. They laid the foundation for all later philosophic thought in Hinduism. Their authors were impatient with the triviality of religion in the Brahmanic period. The Upanishadic prophets looked both within man and into the starry heavens above for a more complete understanding of human life and destiny. They were impatient with the variety of conflicting deities and sought a common or monistic basis of existence. It is easy to suppose that most of the writers of this literature came from groups in Indian society other than the priesthood.

The Upanishads contributed a number of fundamental concepts to later Hinduism, such as *Brahma* (Ultimate Reality), *atman* (the self), *moksha* (deliverance from the chain of finite existence), *samsara* (world of phenomenal existence), *karma* (moral law of causation), and *jnana* (saving knowledge). Both gods and sacrifices fall into the background with the coming of the Upanishads in Hinduism.

Following the Vedic period, whose literature consisted of the Vedas, Brahmanas, and Upanishads, a new stage in the development of Indian history and of Hinduism itself came into being. Many events occurred between the sixth and third centuries B.C. concerning which there is today incomplete knowledge, but of whose meaning for Hinduism there is some clear light. In this period two other significant religious systems, Jainism and Buddhism, were established. The dominant literature in the early part of this period was the *sutras*. These consisted of manuals of ritual and reflected a state of religion prevalent in the age of the Brahmanas. They elaborated the same rites and ceremonies, returned to the old belief in a host of deities, and emphasized an even more vigorous adherence to caste and the four stages of man. It was as though the Upanishads had never been written. The priests of Hinduism had won out.

Politically, too, the period was one of considerable unrest, perhaps reflected in popular Hinduism. At any rate, the country was subject to invasion from without and to changed religious leadership within. King Darius I of Persia occupied the northwestern part of India, where Hinduism was strongest, shortly before 500 B.C. Alexander the Great invaded the Punjab in 326 B.C. The Maurya dynasty, established by Chandragupta around 322 B.C., led eventually to the rule of his Buddhist grandson Asoka between 274 and 232 B.C. Asoka as a Buddhist made Buddhism almost the dominant religion in India, although Hinduism with its remarkable vitality remained and outlasted him.

The Maurya dynasty came to an end in 185 B.C. Following this, northern India was successfully invaded by the Greeks, Sakas, Parthians, and Kushans. The latter were a leading Iranian tribe; their most important king, Kanishka, lived in the second century A.D. The Kushans in turn declined, caught as they were between the rising Sassanian Empire in the west and the Guptas, a new dynasty in India.

The period between the fall of the Mauryan Empire (185 B.C.) and the fall of the Kushans (about 300 A.D.), is traditionally called the epic period. In it, Hinduism underwent renewal. The great Indian epics, the Ramayana and the Mahabharata, were formulated and became influential literature. A part of the Mahabharata, the Bhagavad Gita, became a source of stirring excitment to many Hindu philosophers and religious teachers as well as to many people generally. In this period also the three great sects of Hinduism arose: Vaishnavism, the worship of the god Vishnu or one of his incarnations; Saivism, the worship of the god Siva; and Saktism, the worship of the consorts of Siva. Hinduism spread throughout India and even into Sumatra, Java, Borneo, Malaya, and Indo-China. The authority of the literature and ideas of the previous periods, moreover, became highly accepted and practiced.

Chandragupta I (not to be confused with the previously mentioned Chandragupta) founded the Gupta Empire which ruled most of northern India in 318 A.D. This dynasty continued until the eighth century A.D. Although the Guptas did not attempt to rule southern India, they did encourage the spread of Hinduism throughout southeast Asia. They continued their supremacy until the White Huns, sometimes called the Ephthalites, began a succession of invasions into northwest India, and northern India was eventually divided into a number of small political jurisdictions.

In the Gupta era, Hinduism was remarkably vigorous. Its literature was marked by the production of the Puranas, pious legends about deities and heroes. In this period the striking differences in religious belief and practice between the masses and the intellectual elites became quite pronounced. The masses found their satisfaction in popular religion, which was to a considerable extent the religion of the Brahmanic period. The intellectuals, however, were not content with this type of faith. Over a period of time, and through great speculative effort, they established six orthodox schools of Hindu thought: the Nyaya (logical realism), the Vaiseshika (realistic pluralism), the Samkhya (evolutionary dualism), the Yoga (disciplined meditation), the Mimamsa (investigations of the Vedas), and the Vedanta (the "end of the Vedas"). In the appraisal of a number of reliable students, Hinduism under the Guptas blossomed into its Golden Age.

From the eighth to the fourteenth centuries A.D., Indian society and Hinduism itself were markedly threatened. In a sharp political rivalry northern India was divided between competing Indian powers, and the followers of Islam gained control. Mahmud of Ghazni (998-1030 A.D.) in the tenth century conquered the Punjab. But it was not until the sultanate of Muhammad ibn Tughlak (1325-51) that the full force of Islam was felt throughout a large part of India.

Although Hinduism's vitality was greatly curbed in northern India, by contrast it flourished in the south. There, for example, the philosopher Sankara (788-820? A.D.), contributed mightily to the cogent appeal of the religion. Born a Brahman (member of the highest caste) in North Travancore, he early renounced the world and as a religious teacher traveled throughout India. In his lifetime he established four monasteries which exist even now. His system of philosophy is called Advaita. It is based upon the Upanishads, the Bhagavad Gita, and other traditional scriptures. In his philosophy he sought to disprove the leading thought systems of his time: the Buddhist school of philosophy and such Hindu systems as Samkhya, Yoga, Mimamsa, and Vedanta. He stood strongly for the orthodox Vedic faith and was instrumental in mitigating the influence of the repulsive expressions of Saivism and Saktism. Within Hinduism the contribution of Sankara's Adaita system of philosophy stands as a truly great achievement. From a world perspective his system of thought has been recognized as one of the most comprehensive and profound that the human race has produced. Most Hindus are followers in one way or another of Sankara.

Divided India was reunited in 1526 when the Mughal dynasty was founded by Baber, a descendant of both Tamerlane (Timur Lang) and Jenghiz Khan. Under Akbar (1556-1605 A.D.), most renowned of the Mughal rulers, the Islamic empire achieved its widest geographic coverage. Akbar was a truly great ruler, who succeeded in uniting a number of diverse states, races, and religions into a relatively harmonious whole. In addition, he was a strong advocate of universal tolerance. He himself tried to bring various faiths together into one religion, called Din-i-Ilahi, meaning the "Divine Faith." Never influential during his lifetime, it hardly survived his death.

In the tolerant environment Akbar created in India, Hinduism experienced a revival. A devotional (*bhakti*) movement appeared in northern India in the fifteenth century. It was basically Vaishnavite and was subdivided into groups which worshiped Rama and Krishna, the two incarnations of the Lord Vishnu. Ramananda (d. 1469 A.D.), a leader of the Rama group, advocated the equality of all men in the eyes of God. Caste, color, or creed did not matter. One of his disciples, Kabir (1440-1518 A.D.), a Muslim weaver who similarly preached against caste, is venerated as a saint in Hinduism. He wielded an enormous influence upon Nanak (1469-1538), the founder of Sikhism. Tulsi Das (1532-1623) is another noteworthy advocate of Rama worship. His poem, the Ramayana, based on the adventures of this incarnation of Vishnu, is widely read today, especially among the Hindi-speaking people of northern India.

The devotional (*bhakti*) movement had a second segment, which worshiped Krishna but was divided into two cults: the Radha-Krishna and the Rukmini-Krishna. From the latter tradition came Chaitanya (1485-1533), who, while he made no attempt to create a single or universal religion as Kabir and Nanak did, gave support to the view that caste distinctions were not necessary to Hinduism. The devotional movement caught on rapidly in India and for many decades held the allegiance of great numbers of Hindus. But by the middle of the eighteenth century A.D. it had spent itself, although important traces of it continue in India to this day.

Indian life and Hinduism itself were greatly influenced by contacts with the West. The return of the spice-laden ships of Vasco da Gama to Lisbon in 1499 dates the start of Western influence. For almost a century the Portuguese enjoyed commercial supremacy in India, but by reason or various factors, including the rise of Dutch and British sea power, their empire faded in the first half of the seventeenth century. In the 1600's the Dutch succeeded in establishing themselves at many places in India and enjoyed a lucrative trade, while the East India Company, founded by Englishmen on the last day of the year 1600, became in time the bulwark of Britain's establishment of India as a part of her empire.

British rule in India, which began about 1800, created a basic challenge to the character of Hinduism. Prior to this time, Hinduism was confronted mainly with currents of thought and action which originated largely within India, although influences from beyond its borders should not be minimized. But with the coming of the British, Hinduism was thrown into a welter of ideas and movements originating in far distant parts of the world. The main challenge was laid down by Western civilization, with its political and missionary belief and practices. The modern and largely Western disciplines of history, literature, religion, economics, and politics all encouraged faithful followers of Hinduism to look to the sure foundations of their faith. They were able to exercise this option freely because British rule, unlike that of the Muslim past, was not basically concerned with religious matters. It was fundamentally secular, perhaps contributing the notion of the secular state to the current Republic of India. Hinduism, therefore, was able to take full advantage of freedom in its search for revitalization. To a considerable degree this search was rewarded with success, for today Hinduism is a resurgent religion.

A considerable number of prophetic leaders have contributed to the vitality of modern Hinduism. Of these only a few will be mentioned who are of primary importance to an understanding of Hinduism today.

The present renewal of Hinduism was stimulated in great measure by Ram Mohun Roy (1772-1833). He founded the Brahmo Samaj school of thought. His antagonists were two. First, there were the Hindu teachers (*pandits*) of his time who, with the waning of the devotional movement, had almost smothered Hinduism under the wraps of second-rate philosophy and perfunctory religious rites. Second, there were the Christian missionaries of his day. Against both of these he sought, chiefly in the philosophic tradition within Hinduism and especially in the Upanishads, to reconstruct a Hinduism equal to the times. The school he founded, the Brahmo Samaj, is based upon rational theism. To it many of the leading intellectuals of his time were drawn.

In addition to his theoretical teaching about Hinduism, Ram Mohun Roy was also an advocate of scientific education. He strongly opposed idol worship and many ritualistic practices in Hinduism which were in his opinion unworthy of the religion. He denounced the caste system and brought about the abolition of the burning of widows on the funeral pyres of their husbands (*sati*). Although he was appreciative of new ideas, including even some from the Christian tradition, he never advocated anything other than Hinduism. He did not seek to blend religions systematically, and always considered himself a loyal Hindu. Following his death, however, the Brahmo Samaj, under the talented leadership of Devendranath Tagore (1817-1905), became more nationalistic and lost its Hinduistic details. Keshab Chander Sen (1834-1884), a still later leader of the movement, modified it until it became more Christian than

Hindu. As a result of this development, the Brahmo Samaj broke up into three sectarian groups and its power was greatly reduced.

Swami Dayananda (1824-1883) founded the Arya Samaj. This movement was much more aggressive in its efforts to develop a dynamic type of Hinduism for the masses of India. It sought to define the basic nature of Hinduism, and in so doing claimed that this religion is based upon the Vedas alone. The Arya Samaj was relatively uninterested in Hinduism's literary and religious heritage since the time of Vedas, including the Upanishads. Like the Brahmo Samaj, it opposed idol worship and the caste system. Programatically, moreover, it felt a mission not only to reclaim for Hinduism any Hindus who might have left the faith, but also to convert any who were responsive to it. Today it is strongly nationalistic, thus combining a relatively simple and forceful version of Hinduism with strong feelings about nationhood.

In the same period, another leader arose who formulated a fresh version of the meaning of Hinduism. He was Sri Ramakrishna (1836-1886). This religious leader had no book learning; he was rather impatient with scholarship. To him the experience of religion was paramount. He taught that religion, or Hinduism, does not consist of any one of its historical types, such as Vedism, *bhakti*, or *yoga*. His view of religion was so universal that he was able to assert that all religions are only partial glimpses of the divine, and that a living synthesis was urgent in his time for India and elsewhere. Unlike other modern reformers in Hinduism, however, he never denied his membership in the religion. He accepted all its forces and authority; he fought for all of it. Although his understanding of the nature of Brahma came through worship of an image of Kali, the female goddess of destruction, he was not limited, later, to that particularity for himself or for others.

The life and teachings of Sri Ramakrishna are known in America and Europe through the visits of his favorite disciple, Swami Vivekananda (1863-1902). It was the genius of Vivekananda to apply the teachings of Ramakrishna not only to the essentially religious traditions in Hinduism, but also to the imperative tasks of social welfare. Under his leadership more than a hundred centers in all parts of the world, known as the Ramakrishna Mission, were founded. In Swami Vivekananda the ancient religion of India found newly formulated meaning and a significant dynamic in social service. The views and program of Ramakrishna and his disciple Vivekananda are being currently upheld and strengthened by Professor Sarvepalli Radhakrishnan, author of at least a dozen books on religion and culture and a former President of India.

In more recent years a number of other leaders have arisen within Hinduism. Only three of these will be commented upon briefly. First, Sri Aurobindo Ghose (1872-1950) laid stress upon that exalted state of human consciousness which in his terms should be called the Supermind or the Life Divine. This desirable state of mind is attainable only by those who have been liberated from their finite human consciousness. A principal task of Hinduism, according to Ghose, is that of freeing man from the dragging limitations of human existence. Thus, like others in the long course of Hinduism, he centered his conception of that religion in the idea of deliverance (*moksha*). He also taught that a particular kind of *yoga* is effective in raising life to the sublime realm of consciousness. He taught that deliverance from finiteness does not necessarily take the form of self-negation; rather this realization enables the Life Divine to locate itself within the ordinary thoughts and actions of the faithful and to permeate the whole of the everyday responses of men. This latter concept is called *jivanmukti*, a form of religious experience described in the literature of Vedanta. Ghose in 1910 established a hermitage (*asrama*) in Pondicherry in southern India. Following his withdrawal from society he taught his special type of *yoga*. Many persons came from outside India to benefit from his teachings and practices.

In 1961 the hundredth anniversary of the birth of one of the world's leading poets of modern times, Rabindranath Tagore (1861-1941), was celebrated throughout much of the world. Tagore's contribution was two-sided. First, he possessed a strong sense of social mission. In his later years, he spoke in many parts of the world about his social concerns. He was strongly opposed to aggressive nationalism, believing it to be a heinous crime. He favored the abolition of wars and all human exploitation. The source for these views Tagore found in ancient Hinduism.

Second, Tagore was a poet who through his poetry reinterpreted some of the ancient literature of Hinduism for modern times. He was strongly influenced by the Upanishads and earlier poets in the state of Bengal who described the loves of Radha and Krishna. There is a strong mystical emphasis in his poetry, elements of which are apparent in the nature-mysticism of the past.

Of course, the greatest Hindu of modern times by common assent is Mahatma Gandhi (1869-1948). Some appreciative students of his life believe him to be one of the greatest figures ever to be observed on the human scene. Gandhi took several old doctrines of Hinduism and brought them to bear in creative ways on the contemporary situation. He believed in nonviolence (*ahimsa*). Although nonviolence was accepted as a cardinal virtue among Hindus for several centuries, it had not been applied to life and relationships among groups of peoples and nations. In the past, it has been a tenet in the Hindu's personal credo; Gandhi applied it to every human relationship.

His application of the doctrine to India's quest for freedom is well known. For Gandhi, nonviolence was one means available to men who sought *moksha* or salvation. He taught that no one can perfectly realize himself unless he practices nonviolence perfectly. But it is interesting to note that he himself never claimed to be a perfect embodiment of it. Nevertheless, his countrymen, especially since his death, have been inclined to ascribe to him a generous measure of divinity.

SCRIPTURES

The main source for an authoritative understanding of the historical nature of Hinduism is to be found in the sacred scriptures. These more than any other source provide a vivid and detailed account of the growth of Hinduism and of its present multifarious forms.

They are voluminous. They are not gathered together, as for example in Christianity or Islam, in a single volume. The Hindu scriptures constitute a shelf of volumes. So extensive are the sacred writings that scarcely anyone would wish to claim that he is directly

familiar with them all. All are written in the Sanskrit language.
The scriptures of Hinduism are chiefly bound together chronologically. They do not represent a direct succession of ideas nor do
they reveal a common pattern which can be traced within them
from antiquity to modern times. They are as diverse as Hinduism
itself.

The Hindu scriptures have been grouped by scholars in two
categories, although some authorities consider such a simple classification a distortion. First, there is the *sruti*. The *sruti*, meaning
"that which was heard," corresponds to the concept of revealed
teachings as held in other religions. Second, there is the *smriti*,
meaning "that which is remembered." This corresponds to the
auxiliary literature of other religions. The *scruti* clearly takes precedence over the *smriti*. Both types will be reviewed briefly.

The *sruti* scriptures consist of the Vedas, the Brahmanas, and the
Upanishads. These three are not only the basic scriptures of Hinduism, but also the oldest.

The Rigveda, Yajurveda, Samaveda, and Atharvaveda constitute
the four Vedas, which occur historically in the order named. The
Rigveda consists of a large number of hymns in a form to be
recited. They are organized according to the deities extolled and the
families of seers who have celebrated them. The Yajurveda contains
descriptions of ancient sacrifices, many of which reflect pre-Vedic
times. The Samaveda is much like the Rigveda except for its musical
rendering. The Atharvaveda consist of hymns that reflect the daily
life of the faithful.

Scarcely any common theme can be found in the four Vedas,
unless it be the recognition of the personalized forces of nature. Yet
they have had an influential role in all later Hinduism. They laid
the basis for a common language and grammar, a philosophy or attitude toward the universe; for Indian music, mysticism, ritual practices, and other facets of the Hindu religion.

The Brahmanas as literature stand between the Vedas and the
Upanishads. Often they select a passage from the earlier Vedas
and explicate its meaning. In general they praise what is considered
to be true in the Vedic tradition and condemn its opposite. Already

in the Brahmanas a system of interpreting reality was developing whose influence is strongly evident in the Upanishads. This system taught that reality is one, although a threefold method of understanding it is required: the divine, the natural, and the subjective. The Brahmanas are principally concerned with the fundamental relationship between natural and divine aspects of reality. They seek to understand a process by which these two may be harmonized. Also the Brahmanas, in the process of this harmonization, find significance in subjective religious experience. Probably the stress in the Brahmanas on subjective experience laid a basis for the later Upanishads.

The Upanishads are philosophical writings, sometimes called the Vedanta, which reflect the isolated individual in meditation. Also they connote secret teaching. Possibly the developers of the Upanishadic literature found themselves in disfavor with the priesthood, which clearly gained its power and influence through its supervision of popular or ritualistic religion. The Upanishads testify to a type of faith which is not necessarily grounded in or even respectful of such religion. Viewed from the vantage point of later times, they are seen as the highest development of the Vedic literature. Although they consist of more than a hundred somewhat separate descriptions of philosophy, probably only a dozen or still fewer are of primary importance.

The *smriti*, scriptures auxiliary to the *sruti*, are extremely complex in themselves. Traditionally, they are grouped into five categories: the Vedangas or "limbs" of the Vedas; Dharma Sastras or the codes of law, commentaries, digests, and manuals; Nibandhas or writings devoted to rituals and domestic rites; Puranas, or scriptures of popular Hinduism; and the epics, somewhat different literature from the Puranas but also of great popular import. In addition to these five types of auxiliary literature, there are the Darsanas, pertaining to the six schools of philosophy, the Agamas, scriptures of sectarian groups, and other incidental literature. Each of the *smriti* will be briefly reviewed.

The Vedangas are concerned with a variety of practical matters. No subject seems too unimportant to be included in them, and some topics are of considerable significance. They deal with such matters as etymology, astronomy, grammar, phonetics, and the ritual codes which the priesthood apparently required for its activities. Since early Hinduism placed great stress upon the precise and skilled manner in which hymns were to be sung and sacrifices performed, it required an auxiliary literature which gave detailed instruction regarding correct belief and practice.

The Dharma Sastras consist of regulations and injunctions dealing with a wide range of personal and social subjects. They seek to regulate personal hygiene, the formal relations between people, and even the manner required of faithful Hindus. But the Dharma Sastras also contain detailed instructions on the administration of government and the ways by which justice may be secured in social relations. The Laws of Manu are the most important of the Dharma Sastras. Manu, a patriarchal teacher, laid down regulations governing Hindu behavior which are valued even today.

The Nibandhas consist primarily of writings which provide encyclopedic instruction on most of the major categories of religious and family life.

The Puranas, like the epics shortly to be described, portray the popular forms of Hinduism in imaginative language. They form the materials for storytellers and minstrels, who take ancient and profound scenes from the Vedas and elaborate them for the attention of the masses. The Puranas constitute the latest volume of the total scriptures of Hinduism. Caught up into them are a variety of cultural and practical matters which provide the student of anthropology as well as the historian of Hinduism and of India herself with a rich source for investigation. There is scarcely a subject of human appeal which is not commented upon in the Puranas: how to make and avoid poisons, the use of perfumes, how to detect precious stones, the guidance of celestial bodies for practical human affairs, omens, what proper writing is, the nature of the body, how to farm successfully, and so forth. All these and other topics are found in the midst of exciting stories, some of which involved the activities of Vishnu and Siva.

The Ramayana and the Mahabharata are the two great epics of

Hinduism. Practically all Hindus are familiar with them, since they form the basis for the education of young children in Hindu homes. It is to them that Hindu parents regularly turn when they want to tell bedtime stories.

The Ramayana relates the exploits of Lord Vishnu at great length. Incarnated as Rama, he is always on the side of the good and portrays the victory of good forces over bad. He upholds the sacred ideals by which personal and social conduct are provided with an heroic and moral dimension. He is the kind of king, as Mahatma Gandhi appreciated, who embodied perfect righteousness and truth.

The Mahabharata attempts much more than the Ramayana. More intellectual in its content and persuasive in its unfolding, it is less poetic and more direct in its teaching than the Ramayana. Its central focus is the Bhagavad Gita, considered by many both within Hinduism and outside it as the greatest of all Hindu scriptures. This sonorous poem combines philosophic and devotional content in language of compelling attraction.

While the Vedas are the most authoritative scripture for Hindus, the Bhagavad Gita is probably the most appealing and inspiring. To it countless Indian leaders have turned for inspiration, both general and religious. Its devotional format and spirit cast it as one of India's and the world's foremost documents of devotion. Indicative of the importance of the work is the fact that many noted leaders of Indian life during the last half-century—Aurobindo, Tilak, Nehru, Gandhi, and Radhakrishnan among others—all have written commentaries on the Gita.

The Bhagavad Gita is a complex document despite its relative brevity. Its meaning is not always clear even to those who have studied it. Thus, Tilak concludes that the Gita supports a non-pacifist view of human relations, while Gandhi saw in it the source of his convictions on nonviolence. Similarly the Gita's theological outlook is a combination of pantheism and theism. Essentially, however, the book is concerned with the nature of right action (*dharma*). How can a man act in a proper way, especially in view of the power of self-oriented desire? The Gita constitutes an analysis of the difficulties involved in right action, the role of knowledge in decision-making, and the ideal of perfect surrender to Krishna, who is the embodiment of perfection. Freedom from the blind forces of self and self-desire, then, is offered as the solution. This freedom is secured through union with God, who is Ultimate Reality. By this union the self is purged of its self-centeredness and is further illumined and enraptured by relationship with God. The goal for the human being is not lack of action, but action in harmony with Ultimate Reality.

As noted earlier, Hinduism developed over the centuries six main schools of interpreting the Vedas. All hold that they are the most important records in Hinduism, and each seeks to interpret and support them with derivative arguments. Each has its own interpretive literature. The schools are known as Darsanas or Institutions of Truth, and their respective literature are likewise known as the Darsanas. Since one can scarcely enter directly into a study of the Vedas or of the meaning of Hinduism as a whole, the Darsanas offer the inquirer reasoned passways into the core of traditional Hinduism.

The Agamas are sectarian scriptures. Each of three chief sects in Hinduism—Vaishnavism, Saivism, and Saktism—has its own literary formulations aimed at supplementing the basic or revealed scriptures, the *sruti*. Sometimes the term Tantra is used interchangeably with Agama. The Agamas or Tantras generally discuss philosophical beliefs, meditative exercises, the building of temples, the making of images and their use in worship, and conduct.

In addition to the revealed (*sruti*) and auxiliary (*smriti*) scriptures of Hinduism, there exists a large and ever growing number of respected books, hymns, poems, and devotional writings which explain and give support to one phase or another of Hinduism.

Despite the enormous variety in the sacred scriptures, faithful and knowledgeable Hindus are ever ready to recognize their authority and to seek religious benefits from them. Generally the Hindu is not a skeptic so far as his scriptures are concerned. He may admit that he is not able to describe them systematically; in fact, he may not be technically aware of their full range. But he is responsive to those he knows. He is open-minded toward their claims upon him.

He depends upon and utilizes what he knows of them. Hinduism is
a religion that depends heavily upon its sacred scriptures.

TEACHINGS

The previous sections on history and the sacred scriptures of
Hinduism have already given some information as to the teachings
of the religion. An historical description has the advantage of por-
traying the development of doctrine. Other approaches, however,
such as the comparative, scriptural, philosophical, theological, or
systematic, have their own contributions to make. It is appropriate,
therefore, now to describe in a systematic fashion the nature of the
teachings or beliefs of Hinduism. These will be discussed under
three headings: God, the person, and society. The use of these
categories, however, should not obscure the fact that the teachings
of Hinduism, like those of any religion, are actually not restricted
to exclusive categories. Its teachings on God, the person, and society
in reality blend or interpenetrate. One may start with an element in
one category and before long find that its ramifications take one
throughout the others. Yet for the purpose of relatively simple
presentation the three headings are useful.

In Hinduism, intellectual assent is not a matter of supreme importance. Actually, as must be apparent from the previous discussion,
it is a faith based primarily on experience. It does not find its
uniqueness in the acceptance of academic abstractions, but in the
response of the individual and the community to Divine Reality.
Religious experience, according to Hinduism, does not need to be
intellectually defended. It stands on its own two feet. No matter
how its rationalization may differ from that given to the religious
experience of others, it is self-certifying. Thus within Hinduism
may be found a variety of religious experiences, each of which is
viewed as essentially sacred and inviolate. One Hindu does not
condemn the religious experience of another simply because it differs radically from his own. Critical faculties are used, indeed, but
rather as the means of relating partial truth to the total Truth.
Essentially the Hindu attitude of trust toward diverse beliefs and

forms of religion enables him to admit that points of view other than his own are entirely worthy of consideration and acceptance. Because of this flexibility and trustfulness, it is difficult to speak about orthodoxy and heresy in Hinduism.

Another warning bell must be rung for the non-Hindu. Each religion has its own key concepts which are expressed commonly by key words. These often do not have exact synonyms in English. For example, *dharma* in Sanskrit is regularly translated as "law" in English, but actually they are not quite the same. Similarly *jati* usually is translated as "caste," but has connotations to the Hindu which are different from those that occur to a non-Hindu. What is true of Hindu words holds also, of course, for the special words of other religions. Thus it is particularly difficult to translate such words as "charity" and "cross" from Christianity into language suitable to the understanding of the Hindu.

But words alone are not the full difficulty. There is another tendency which requires attention. The mind of each person is so filled with meanings given to words and concepts within his own tradition that he almost automatically runs into the danger of reading into other people's words and concepts those with which he is familiar. The non-Hindu has a built-in tendency to convert Hindu concepts and meanings into his own.

Even the earnest Hindu thinker is not able directly and comprehensively to understand the whole of Hinduism. He finds it necessary to depend upon one or more of the six systems of philosophy that developed in India. Some understanding of these points of view or schools of thought may prove helpful in understanding Hindu doctrines. Although the six are seemingly contradictory at some points and genuinely opposed at others, Hindus think of them as complementary to each other. They remind one of the experiences of the seven blind men feeling the elephant in the popular Buddhist fable (also found in other Indian religions). Each one believes himself to have some knowledge of the whole.

Actually more than the six traditional systems of Hindu thought have sprung up over the many years from the beginning of the religion until these systems were finally formed and fixed. But the six are usually accepted by Hindu scholars as being thoroughly representative of the larger number. Moreover, like the others, they have one feature in common: they all possess authority by reason of their connection with the Vedas. Essentially they do not seek to be independent systems; each readily acknowledges its reliance upon the original sacred scriptures of Hinduism. By the time of the six systems, however, the religion based on the Vedas accepted as scripture the Brahmanas and the Upanishads, since these were considered invaluable commentaries and interpretations of the Vedas themselves.

Of the systems or schools of philosophy named earlier, Nyaya and Vaiseshika form one group; Samkhya and Yoga are highly related; while Mimamsa and Vedanta are closer to each other. This order of mention does not reflect the chronological order in which the systems were founded, but rather their relationships to each other as they finally developed.

The Nyaya is chiefly concerned with logical methods. The Vaiseshika, on the other hand, discusses the nature of the world. Each school, however, accepts the findings of the other. The Nyaya readily accepts the conclusions of the Vaiseshika regarding the atomistic nature of the world, while the Vaiseshika arrives at its conception of the world by using the logical methods of the Nyaya. According to the Nyaya there are four sources of knowledge: perception (*pratyakasha*), inference (*anumana*), analogy (*upamana*), and credible testimony (*sabda*). Some scholars have been impressed with the similarity of the methods employed in the Nyaya school and the syllogistic analysis of Aristotle.

The Nyaya school may be divided into two historical periods. Gautama (not the Gautama of Buddhism) introduced his Nyaya Sutra in the third century B.C. This document constitutes one of the earliest known efforts of an extended and systematic nature to describe proper ways of thinking. The second period began with the introduction by Gangesa of Mithila (1200 A.D.) of his Tattvacintamani, the standard text of the school in its modern phase. Gangesa's main effort lay in being even more precise about methods of thinking than his predecessors.

The Vaiseshika devotes itself primarily to the composition of the universe. This school teaches that all material objects are composed of four kinds of atoms: earth, water, fire, and air. These atoms in different combinations make up different materials. Yet the Vaiseshika is not a materialistic philosophy. It teaches that in actuality there are nine fundamental or atomic substances. In addition to the four kinds of material atoms there are the following components of reality: space, time, ether (*akasa*), mind, and soul. The Vaiseshika school bases its teachings upon a personal God who created the world out of the nine substances. These substances antidated God, but his task was to shape them into an ordered universe. Thus God is the creator of the world, but a special meaning attaches to his action. The Vaiseshika system recognizes Kanada (about the third century B.C.) as the innovator of the school through the production of his Vaiseshika Sutra.

The third school, that of Samkhya, looks to Kapila as its founder. It is a very old system, dating to the seventh century B.C., and important because it contributed so many basic categories to philosophical Hinduism. Samkhya teaches that there are two basic elements which comprise the universe: the *purusha* and the *prakriti*. These are viewed dualistically. The *purusha* refers to nonmaterial factors —the selves and spirits, for example. The *prakriti* largely represents objective existence. The Samkhyan conception of the realm of nature is indeed broad; it includes both the material and the psychical. Nature is conceived both as existence and potentiality. The world is in a complex process of evolution. The *prakriti* forms the fundamental substance which is influenced by the *purusha*. All natural and human history is a consequence of the interaction of these two elements. The evolution is not erratic or accidental; it is a result of the principle of causation. Causes and effects, according to the Samkhya school, are evident in all change. While they are distinct entities, the effect is always present in the cause. The effect is a different arrangement of the cause by reason of the contribution of the *purusha*.

Various stages can be identified in evolution. The first is characterized by the development of the intellect (*buddhi*), which is considered to be worthy or great (*mahat*). Following this stage is that of the ego. The ego represents a higher state in that awareness of the self as a whole involves more factors than intellect. At later stages the five cognitive organs, the five motor organs, and the disciplined mind come into being.

The aim of life, according to the Samkhyan system, is the emancipation of the self from the bondage of the body. A knowledge of the difference between the self and the body is essential to emancipation, and an understanding of the relationships between *purusha* and *prakriti* assists in the process. The mature person is one who is able to make this important distinction. His self is no longer bound by the *prakriti*. He becomes removed in life from the control of ordinary events, and at death is truly emancipated by being free from rebirth.

Some persons have described the Samkhyan philosophy as basically atheistic. Its founder Kapila, it is true, did not find it necessary to assume the existence of God. Yet he did not deny it. Seemingly his effort was to show that God's existence cannot be satisfactorily and finally proved by any sort of evidence. Later the Samkhyan school accepted the existence of God.

The *yoga* school, fourth of the six, is probably more familiar in the West than the others. Unlike the Samkhyan system, which depends upon knowledge to lead to the freedom of the self, Yoga teaches that such freedom can be secured by the discipline of both the mind and the body. The Yoga system, moreover, is not particularly strong in its teachings about the nature of the universe; it is more of an instrumentality by which the state of freedom of the self may be achieved than a philosophy of the universe. Much has been written on the subject of *yoga*, and there is no common agreement as to its nature. Historically it has been outlined in the Bhagavad Gita, and Patanjali (a second century B.C. author of the Yoga Sutras) is considered the principal systematizer of the subject.

The practice of *yoga* consists of eight types of discipline: abstentions, obligations, postures, breath control, abstraction, concentration, meditation, and absorption.

The abstentions are from lying, theft, violence, sensual satisfaction, and the acceptance of gifts. The begging bowl is no part of *yoga*. The obligations are to ascetic practices, study of the scriptures, contemplation of the laws, cleanliness, and contentment. The postures are not of primary importance in themselves; they are a means to an end, engaged in to subdue the body and make it possible for the self to participate motionlessly in worship and meditation for long periods of time. Similarly breath control (*pranayama*) is practiced as a means of controlling the body and attaining supersenuous states. Abstraction, concentration, and meditation also are means (of a higher order than the postures and breath control) enabling the worshiper to achieve union with Ultimate Reality. In the higher efforts, the self undergoes visions and mystical experiences which, it is thought, release him from disabilities carried over from his previous birth. These make him secure from the evils of old age, disease, and even death. Through the practice of *yoga* in all its stages, the appeals of the lower life can be resisted and the body itself can be transformed in vitality and power.

The practice of *yoga* is not easy. The eight disciplines depend upon a highly controlled will. Usually a long period of time is required to realize the superconscious state. Indeed, a whole lifetime of practice can easily be devoted to Yoga. Although many in the West practice it as a means of bodily improvement, its larger meaning in Hinduism requires the careful control and subjection of the body to the higher or spiritual goals of the religion. To the Hindu, Yoga is a principal means of emancipation (*moksha*).

The Mimamsa point of view is found in the Mimamsa Sutra, written or composed by Jaimini (about 400 B.C.). This Sutra is a work of practical scholarship. The Mimamsa School, based primarily upon an investigation of the Vedas, holds that in the study of the Vedas there is the possibility of understanding the true nature of Hinduism. Hinduism in this context tends to be a corollary of right action (*dharma*). In a sense, Mimamsa is a school of interpreting the Vedas for practical action rather than a contemplative or speculative system of thought.

The Vedanta is primarily philosophical in its intent and is quite possibly the most influential of all the philosophical systems within

Hinduism. The system is based upon a number of documents. Badarayana, Vedanta's founder, contributed the Brahma Sutra. The Upanishads and the Bhagavad Gita comprise the other chief resources of the school.

Gudapada, who taught a rigid form of monism, forcefully stressed the unreality of the external world. The only reality is Brahma, the deity expounded in the Upanishads. According to Gaudapada, dreams and subjective experiences are highly similar. Only Brahma truly exists; all else is fancy and illusion.

Sankara, however, is the most noted teacher of the Vedanta school. Living in south India in the eighth century A.D., he took a less extreme position than Gaudapada. He believed that Brahma is identical with the human self (atman). He also denied the independent nature of the external. Yet he did not go so far as to think of the world as pure illusion. External objects do have an authentic form of existence. Its nature is explained by Sankara in this way: anyone may mistake a rope for a serpent. In such circumstances, it is not possible to say that the rope does not exist. One only can say that the rope is not a serpent. The illusion of the serpent disappears as soon as the rope is carefully investigated. In this analogy, the world is the serpent and Brahma the rope. True knowledge is secured when the world is recognized as only a manifestation of Brahma. The world is simply an appearance, neither real nor unreal, sustained by the existence of Brahma. Brahma is the basic existence. The world is what it is through its relationship to Brahma. If the world were not to exist, Brahma still would exist, but since Brahma is not an empirical form, knowledge of Brahma depends upon observable events in the external world.

The soul of the individual person (jiva) is an expression of Brahma. Ignorance (avidya) is the root cause of all human problems. The self or ego exists to overcome ignorance and to be united with Brahma. Such deliverance is the goal of human living. If it is attained in the person's lifetime, he is fully realized or liberated (jivanmukta).

Actually, there are two main divisions in the Vedanta school. That of Sankara is strictly nondualistic (advaita). The other is essentially dualistic (*dvaita*). Ramanuja and Madhva, leading Vaishnava scholars, are the leading advocates of dualistic systems. Ramanuja claimed that the world and Brahma are distinct, though not separate. Everything and everyone exist in and for Brahma. But a degree of separation is maintainable between the created world and the creator.

Madhva taught in the thirteenth century A.D., two centuries after Ramanuja. He believed in the thorough separation of Brahma and individual souls (*jiva*). The appropriate designation for his philosophy is *dvaita*. In it, individual souls and the external world both truly exist. But in the various and recognizable levels of existence, Brahma is the highest reality. Madhva was a principal contributor to the Vaishnava cult or movement.

These six schools contain points of continuity and distinction. They are viewed by many Hindus as offering separate but complimentary ways of understanding Hinduism. Followers of the particular schools are tolerant toward each other, recognizing that each has its contribution to make.

God

The teaching of Hinduism regarding God is probably more complex than that of any other living religion. No single statement may be made on the subject with sureness that it will be complete. Hinduism offers as many deities, in number and kind, as probably have been conceived in world history. Some explication will make these statements more understandable.

The divine in Hinduism has been described in pluralistic, dualistic, and monistic terms. The Nyaya, Vaiseshika, and Yoga schools of thought, for example, teach pluralistic theism. In their view, God did not create the world out of nothing. He created it out of preexisting materials or he created it out of himself. This doctrine means that while God is in a sense one, he is surrounded by many other alternate realities. Again, in the Vedic tradition many deities are recognized as well as their consorts. There is, for example, the Hindu Triad or Trinity: Brahma, Vishnu, and Siva. Brahma, the creator, is linked to Sarasvati, the goddess of speech and learning. Vishnu, the protector, has Lakshmi, goddess of wealth and prosperity, as his consort. Siva, the destroyer, is linked to Sakti, goddess of power and destruction. Vishnu, furthermore, is portrayed in Hinduism as being incarnate in human form on several occasions when grave evils are present in the world. Rama and Krishna are regarded as incarnations (*avatars*) of Vishnu. As such, they are also worshiped by all Hindus.

A dualistic conception of the deity is also found in Hinduism. The dualistic theism of Madhva has been explained: for him, in summary, there are two ultimate forms of reality. Brahma is the absolute upon which all else depends, but the external world and the self are relative realities. Although all realities are related and may be placed in an order of worth, they are, in fact, distinct. There are traces of monism in Madhva's philosophy in that he makes everything continguent upon Brahma. Yet there also are traces of pluralism in that God is also called by many names other than Brahma—such as Narayana, Vishnu, and Hari.

Monistic theism is evident in the teachings of many Hindus, including Sankara, mentioned above, who opposed dualistic philosophy (*dvaita*). He believed that Brahma is not completely different from the self and the external world. Yet his monism is qualified in that he was able to accord some measure of independent reality to the self and the world. In his view, however, Brahma is the only absolute and independent reality. As the Supreme Being, Brahma provides existence and meaning to all else.

Numerically, Ultimate Reality in Hinduism has been described as the many, the two, and the one; but the deities may be considered in other dimensions as well. They may be described as superpersonal, personal, and impersonal. Theism basically is the belief in a personal Being who is capable of an understanding and responsive relationship between himself and his creatures. But there are systems of thought in Hinduism which deny the validity of any personal attributes by which God might be described. The monistic system of Sankara is such a system. Sankara taught that Brahma is the sole and absolute Reality. External reality exists, but Brahma is pure existence. He cannot be described or understood in terms of personal qualities. In fact, Brahma should be spoken of as "It." Any assertion about him can properly be denied—his consciousness, purpose, or feelings. He is the God above all Gods. The monism of Sankara, therefore, may be described as supertheistic or superpersonal.

The divine in Hinduism also has been described in personal terms. The teachings of the Nyaya, Vaiseshika, and Yoga schools, to employ familiar examples, hold such a view. No matter what differences the adherents of these schools may ascribe to real and unreal relationships between God, the self, and the world, there is the ready assurance that God is theistically or personally conceived. God, according to this view, thinks, feels, and acts. It is he who created the world out of preexisting materials. His purpose fulfilled this task. The preexisting materials did not possess a consciousness or purpose by which they could fashion the ordered world out of themselves. As a person who formed the world and all that is therein, this God or Brahma is not absolutely removed from all human categories and relationships.

Hinduism also teaches that the divine is impersonal. The Samkhya, previously explained, is a dualistic system which accounts for the nature of man and the universe without recourse to belief in a personal God. According to this philosophy, there are two ultimate realities which exist independently of each other: *purusha* and *prakriti*.

Evolution was started, as it is maintained, by the contact and relationship between these two impersonal principles. Each is accorded a highly independent existence and acts without that degree of consciousness and purpose which traditionally has been ascribed to persons, both human and divine. No third principle or person, such as God, is taught in Samkhya. Thus, no one Being ties the whole of reality together and interprets it to human kind as a relationship essentially between personal entities.

Historically and contemporarily Hinduism, aside from Brahma, proffers several major deities. Vishnu and Siva are important in large part because they are affiliated with cults which recognize and support them.

Vishnu is considered the protector and sustainer of the world. He is worshiped in the major cult of Vaishnavism, popular in all sections of India. The concept of Vishnu has attracted other deities to it in the long course of its development, such as the cosmic god Narayana, of the Vedas and the Brahmanas.

One important attribute of Vishnu is his love of right action (*dharma*). He supports the notion in Hinduism that one should do his duty without expecting any reward. Stories of his righteousness inspire many Hindus with adoration and the stimulus to emulate him.

Vishnu is also characterized by his different forms. Hinduism teaches that he has on innumerable occasions incarnated himself in the world of men and animals. For example, he is said to have incarnated himself as a great tortoise in order to sustain the world on his back, and as a man-lion in order to kill a demon who plotted to kill his own son. He has also taken the form of human beings. As Rama he represents Indian manhood at its noblest, his exploits in the service of justice embodied in epic form in the Ramayana, and this expression of Vishnu is worshiped exclusively by some Hindus. So devoted are some of his followers that they worship Rama's wife, Sita—model of self-sacrificing womanhood—his brother Lakshmana, and even his monkey servant, Hanuman.

Krishna is another incarnation of Vishnu. His activities are described in the Mahabharata and in the Bhagvata Purana. He is depicted in Hinduism in several stages of his life—as a sweet infant dancing in glee, as the divine youth playing on a flute, or as a charioteer in war. In most of his portrayals he gives expression to the divine character of love, although justice is also a part of his make-up. The worship of Vishnu is especially strong in India and is supported by several festivals and thousands of shrines scattered throughout the country.

Siva also is an important deity in Hinduism. Like Vishnu he combines in himself a number of attributes which probably are derived from other deities and experiences in the history of Hinduism. Primarily he is the god of destruction. But he not only destroys, he creates and sustains. There is a strong sense of his specially creative ability in the cult which places him at the center of its worship. The great god Siva has revealed himself in three primary forms: animal, anthropomorphic or human, and phallic. Siva temples, for example, feature a representation of a sacred bull which is Siva in his animal form. This bull is a reminder that Siva is present with the worshipers in animal form.

Siva also has revealed himself in human forms. Although these forms of Siva are not usually the principal objects of worship within the Siva cult, they are highly venerated. Siva, according to the cult, has taken many human forms and has performed roles from heroism in warfare to the punishing of Brahma for telling lies.

The Siva *linga* (phallus) also is an object of veneration. The *linga* apparently was an object of worship of the ancient Hindus. There is strong condemnation of it in the Vedic literature, which negatively proves its early existence. Probably the worship of the *linga* was supported by feelings of awe and respect toward the creative principle in life itself. At any rate, *linga* representations are everywhere found in the cult of Siva.

Siva's active power or *sakti* is expressed in female form in the worship of the various consorts of the deity. Thus, Saktism, while primarily related to the worship of Siva, becomes in northern India, for example, almost a separate phase of Hinduism. Saktism takes essentially two forms. In the first or the "right-hand" form it emphasizes the benign or positive features of nature's energy. The second or the "left-hand" type stresses the natural impulses of man and nature. It issues in secret ceremonies in which human restraints are lifted.

These deities, as well as others, bear a relationship to Brahma. Brahma is the One Reality who is pure existence. Brahma is not directly discoverable, but he reveals himself, superpersonal though he may be, in a variety of divine forms. These divine forms are the more evident and sometimes personal manifestations of Brahma. He is usually, therefore, not the object of cult worship. He—or it—is the primal assumption behind everything, including the partial glimpses of him as expressed in the conceptions and activities of Vishnu, Siva, and the other Hindu deities.

The Person

The individual life of the Hindu is influenced by his religion. The teachings of Hinduism concerning the person have been formulated in a number of ways. The organization of personal life into four stages constitutes a widely accepted view. These stages are: the student (*brahmacharya*), the householder (*garhasthya*), the hermit or recluse (*vanaprasthya*), and the ascetic (*sannyasa*). Each of these will be commented upon briefly.

The chief goals of the first stage are the acquisition of knowledge, the building of character, and preparation for those responsibilities which are a part of family and community life. The student begins this period somewhere between the eighth and the twelfth year with a rite of initiation. A teacher is chosen in whose home he must live while devoting himself solely to the aims of his studentship. In the rite the student approaches the teacher with a sacred twig. By this gesture he indicates his willingness to obey his teacher. In former times the responsibility for the student was given to the community. He supported himself by begging from the community, although he was not required to pay fixed fees to his teacher. By this arrangement, student and teacher were relatively independent of the student's family, and education itself was not dependent upon the family's wealth or lack of it. It was highly individualized and involved no prescribed course of study; each student was able to learn at his own pace. In recent years such educational practice has been modified somewhat, although ritually the stage of life is honored. At the end of this period the student undergoes a ceremonial bath. By this act he passes on to the householder stage.

The second or householder stage is initiated by marriage, which obviously introduces a person into adult and responsible life. The first stage is the preparation for the second.

Marriage in Hinduism is a sacrament—that is, not a contract but a religious obligation. Through marriage and the creation of children the family line is continued and the important social institution of the family maintained. The family, moreover, provides the training ground for the individual's participation in community activities.

The family in Hinduism is clearly not a secular arrangement alone. This faith enjoins the householder to perform five basic sacrifices as an expression of his religious obligation. These are: Vedic study, the daily offering of water to the forefathers, devotional offerings to the gods in the sacred fire maintained in the home, the offering of food to all beings, and the offerings of sacrifice through hospitality to men. By these duties the religious tone of the Hindu family is maintained.

Theoretically the role of the woman in Hinduism is the same as for the man. Almost none of the philosophical statements regarding the nature of the self in relation to the Absolute contain any particular distinction between man and woman.

Practically speaking, however, the woman in Hinduism finds her place and fulfillment in relation to her husband and their children. A woman looks to her husband for spiritual guidance and practical advice. Household duties properly fall within her province of responsibility, but in all things she is dependently related to her husband. This view of the role of the woman places her in a subsidiary status. Yet Hinduism has long taught respect for the worth and freedom of women.

In the third stage the person withdraws from active life and becomes a hermit. He casts aside his responsibilities to family and society and takes up residence in the forest, although he may be accompanied by his wife if she also enters into this stage. Together they engage in contemplation, study of the scriptures, and various religious practices aimed at the improvement of their personal existence (*moksha*). Not all Hindus, of course, are able to enter the third stage, since they are obliged to remain in the second by reason of family and community responsibilities.

In the fourth stage asceticism is the rule. The person severs his relation with the world and by solitude and renunciation seeks mystical union with the divine. He is then called a *sannyasin*. As such he seeks to lose the consciousness of self, and through discipline works to realize his spiritual freedom. Again, not all Hindus are able to enter into the ascetic stage.

The four stages in the development of the personal life of the Hindu are based upon a conception of life which is both material and spiritual. This has been recognized by Hindu thinkers as based upon four fundamental human needs: knowledge and maturity, property and association, social continuity and activity, and personal and spiritual realization. Hindu teaching requires that all four of these needs be gratified for the attainment of proper personal development. Together they comprise a blending of material and spiritual factors. Also, Hinduism puts the same substance into different words when it teaches that the loyal Hindu is obligated by three debts. First, he owes much to the Divine Being and is obligated to acknowledge his supremacy and dedicate his life to him. Second, he is indebted to the teachers and seers who have brought him the truths of his tradition. He may meet this obligation by maintaining the religious heritage which he has received. Third, he owes much to his ancestors. This debt he repays through the establishment of a good family, especially with at least one son.

A number of important concepts in Hinduism help to explain the proper attitude and role of the believer. One of these is *dharma*. This, as we have seen, is right action. In the Rig Veda stress is placed upon the right order of the universe, and *dharma* also means that which maintains the order appropriate to a being. Thus, every form of life has its *dharma*, which signifies conformity with the essential truth of things. It pertains to all phases of natural and human life.

Hinduism seeks by means of *dharma* to relate the eternal and the temporal in a regulated and meaningful code of life, which does not imply a denial of human freedom, as some suppose; rather it declares that true freedom is found in appropriate action. License means freedom which does not take into account the *dharma* or right action required in the situation.

Hinduism also teaches a belief in rebirth or, as it is popularly called, transmigration of the soul. Such a doctrine assumes the permanence of the self. If the individual is not essentially eternal in his being, there would be no possibility of speaking of reincarnation. The teaching of rebirth lays great stress upon human worth and is based upon the acceptance of the possibility of individual emancipation (*moksha*). From one perspective the individual always has possessed his real nature. Yet from another perspective the individual is limited by ignorance from self-realization. Some persons may be able within a lifetime, particularly through discipline, to succeed in gaining union with the divine. But for most people such union, although striven for, is not attainable within human experience. The belief in rebirth, therefore, provides every individual with the clear assurance that ultimately the prospect of liberation is an authentic option.

The doctrine of *karma* is another fundamental teaching of Hinduism. It constitutes the law of actions and their retribution. According to the teachings of Hinduism, the law of causation is as evident in the moral as in the physical sphere. Morally the actions of individuals lead inevitably to good or bad results. Every individual in acting understands that the law of *karma* is operative—that is, he will be rewarded according to the quality of his actions. No action ends neutrally. Since the law of *karma* operates inexorably for all human individuals, Hinduism teaches that not all the consequences of an individual's actions are rewarded in this life (as indeed seems obvious from the evidence). Hinduism teaches, therefore, that each individual possesses a series of lives so that the consequences of all his actions may be fulfilled. Thus the doctrine of rebirth, tied as it is to *dharma* and to the law of *karma*, is essential for the maintenance of the ethical theory of Hinduism.

Karma does not lessen man's freedom. It is not an external power, such as fate or destiny, but is in fact a support to individual freedom. For it impresses a person with the self-induced results of his actions. Also, since the individual has freedom, he is able through a succession of lives, as well as in the present life, to better his circumstances by so acting in each and every moment of time as to establish the prospect of positive rewards.

In modern Hinduism, as in the past, three ways are presented to a person by which he may reach God: knowledge (*jnana*), action (*karma*), and devotion (*bhakti*). Some strands of the religion lay primary stress upon one; others advocate other means. So far as one of the three elements predominates in the religious experience and aspiration of the individual, his resulting religious expressions will be shaped accordingly. Yet no one of the three wholly accounts for the full nature of the teachings of Hinduism concerning the person. This religion presents an organized way of life for the individual, although its details are so loosely held as to make room for considerable flexibility and tolerance.

Society

Like other religions, Hinduism is not a mere set of philosophical abstractions. It is a social system determining and determined by the long course of Indian history, expressed in manifold forms in sacred writings, and represented now, as in the past, by diverse and highly developed schools of thought. It has a set of ritualistic patterns employed mainly by individual Hindus, a code of conduct regulating the whole of personal life and social relations, and finally, a socio-religious order in which the many elements of Hinduism are concretely embodied.

The teachings of Hinduism regarding society cover many topics, three of which have been selected for brief treatment: family, village, and caste. Some comments have been made above on the Hindu family, in connection with the four stages of individual life. Additionally it may be said that the Hindu family is a monogomous and patrilineal system. Sometimes it is called a joint family system. These terms mean that commonly the family consists of three generations living together in a dwelling place. The eldest living male member is the chief authority within the group. Even the ancestors of its various living members are regarded as still living within the family, and special recognition is given to them in family ceremonies.

Although the members of joint families live in a single dwelling place, the family subunits usually possess their own living quarters. However, they share together a common kitchen, joint property, and family rights. The Hindu home generally is a very religious place, since there are rituals that must be performed in the early morning, in the middle of the day, and in the evening. In addition, the devout Hindu's life is punctuated from beginning to end with a series of ritualistic celebrations marking off the stages of personal development. For example, there are the "fetus-laying rites" performed at the time of marriage; the rite of supplication for a male child, usually performed in the mother's third month of pregnancy; the blessing of the child's birth; the ceremony ten or twelve days later in which the child's name is given; and the dedication of the child to God four months after his birth.

Marriage is a socially necessary as well as a religiously sacred responsibility for both men and women. A family may be disgraced in the eyes of neighbors if it fails to marry off a daughter by the time she is three years beyond the age of puberty. To avoid disgrace, her family has the basic responsibility to take the initiative. Her father by one means or another proposes marriage to the family— including the prospective bridegroom—into which he would like his daughter to be married. Usually some form of dowry accompanies the marriage.

Although the custom of child marriage is widely known in India, its nature requires understanding. In this case the marriage ceremony is divided into two parts. The first, following betrothal, may be viewed as something like an engagement party in Western society. When the girl reaches the age of puberty and is ready to join her husband's household, a second ceremony takes place. This corresponds roughly to the Western marriage ceremony. Traditionally, marriages across caste lines were forbidden, although today they are legally sanctioned. Where they take place today, however, they usually involve family as well as ritual difficulties of a serious sort.

Child marriages are today on the decrease in India. In part this change results from the changing attitude toward caste. Very early marriage arrangements were desirable in former days when the need for marrying within one's caste or subcaste was more intensely felt. Today, with lessening emphasis on caste, the necessity for child marriage has diminished somewhat. Even where the custom is still practiced in India, it is increasingly approved that the final consummation of marriage should await puberty.

Child marriage is related to the special status of widows and especially of child widows. According to the Code of Manu, virgin child-brides who are widowed may not remarry. Many in this status, therefore, are obliged to spend a lifetime in the husband's family in the role of a servant. Widowers, however, may remarry, although it is often difficult for them to find wives of their own age, since they are not always able to effect a contract with a suitable widow.

Hinduism permits divorce on various grounds, but traditionally it has frowned on easy divorce, and divorce is not widely practiced in India. Perhaps the major reason for it historically has been the failure of the wife to produce offspring, especially sons, who are important in the Hindu family since great stress is placed upon family continuity. The Indian family has been a social factor of the highest importance in maintaining the social equilibrium and personal security of the peoples of India.

The village is another important element of social security. In the recent decades there has been a marked trend toward urbanization, yet the country—both modern Pakistan and India proper— is still predominantly rural. Perhaps as many as 70 per cent of the people even now are directly related to agriculture. No one knows exactly how many villages there are in India and Pakistan, but a suggestion has been made that there are at least 550,000 in India alone. Thus still today the village is a preeminent fact in Indian life.

Villages are generally organized on the basis of ingroup relations. Since caste plays a determining role in Indian life, the village, for the sake of efficiency if not for other reasons, is based primarily upon acceptable caste relationships.

Its formal organization and administration are not democratic as this term is understood in the West. Relationships and events are governed informally by the village owners. These in turn are highly influenced or even controlled by customary patterns and practices. The principal concerns of village leaders are: wells, cowpens, groves, and reservoirs. Considerable independence, self-sufficiency, and even autonomy characterize Indian villages. However, the impact of Western ideas and practices regarding agriculture, government, and other matters, as well as the increasingly active functions of the national government of India, formed as it is by Western culture, are increasingly modifying the traditional village life and organization.

The villages are religiously significant. An ordinary villager in India would largely lack any clear understanding of the formal aspects of Hinduism presented in this chapter. There is a great gulf fixed between the religion of the villager and that of the Brahman villager, the priest of Hinduism. The villager believes in animism —that natural objects possess a soul. He has respect for the shaman, the medicine man or wonder-worker who is thought to be able to influence supernatural powers. He believes in fetishes—material objects deemed to have magical potency. His religion is primitive or unsophisticated. In fact, it may properly be claimed that in some places in India village religion has virtually supplanted Hinduism as formally described in this chapter.

On the other hand, village animism often exists side by side in the same place with the higher forms of Hinduism. Thus, a village may have shrines for the worship of the great gods of Hinduism—shrines administered by Brahmans—while it also has other shrines devoted to the special village spirits.

The villager usually adopts some spirit as his own, and for his family. To it he pays homage at dawn and at dusk. But he is also keenly appreciative of all deities everywhere. He will feel free to call upon any one of them as his need arises. And he is not distrustful of the services performed by the priests, whether these take place in his own home or at a shrine.

The villager also finds deep religious satisfaction in pilgrimages, of which many holy places in India are the object. The river Ganges —"Mother Ganges," as pious Indians would call it—is perhaps the holiest, especially at Benares. This sacred river is believed to have power to release a person from sin and disease. To die in it means assurance of Siva's heaven.

The villager, as indeed the great mass of city-dwelling Hindus also, has great respect for cows. This is religiously based, since the cow is traditionally considered of all animals the most sacred. Even Gandhi deemed "cow-protection" to be "the central fact of Hinduism." He felt that the reverence shown to cows reflected the Indian's respect for the entire subhuman world. A villager would be no less wholehearted in the matter. At certain times of year, cows are honored as gods. They are dressed in garlands, annointed with oil and water, and gratefully admired by the villagers. In times past the killing of a cow was a capital offense, and even now cow dung is believed to possess disinfectant and medicinal powers.

The teachings of Hinduism on the organization of society in the caste system are of first importance in understanding the nature of both the faith itself and of Indian society. The organization of the life of the individual into four stages is called *asramadharma* in Hinduism, while the caste system is considered the parallel or counterpart for society. It is called *varnadharma*. Together they comprise the teachings of Hinduism regarding the individual and society.

Caste is an extremely complex as well as important concept. It resists easy definition. Theoretically Indian society has been divided into four major caste groups, each of which contains numerous subcastes within it. The major castes are: the Brahmans, or the priestly, intellectual caste; the Kshatriyas, the warrior and ruling caste; the Vaisyas, the primarily commercial and agricultural caste; and the Sudras, the agricultural and artisan caste. In actuality, however, there is a fifth caste. It is composed of those persons who for one reason or another do not fit into the theoretical system. These are termed outcastes, untouchables, Panchamas, Harijans, or the "scheduled" class. The three highest castes, beginning with the Brahmans, are known as the twice-born. By this is meant that they have passed through the sacrament of initiation which is their second birth.

Caste is fundamentally endogamous. A Hindu does not select a caste for himself; he is born into one. Marriage beyond the caste, while legally permitted, is not followed. The nature of caste, therefore, places severe limitations upon both horizontal and vertical movement within Indian society. Each caste possesses a common name and serves at particular occupations. Reverence for a common origin, supported by venerated myth and the obligation to perform ritual practices required by the individual caste, tend to support its ingroup character. Thus each caste regulates its own life by principles and practices peculiar to it. Each remains separate from all other castes, although each maintains formalized relationships with others.

Some scholars have claimed that the caste system originated when the light-skinned Aryans invaded the northern part of India several thousands of years ago, finding there the dark-skinned indigenous peoples. The Sanskrit word for caste is *varna,* a term which denotes color. These scholars think that the Aryan invaders invented the caste system and gave it religious support as a means of subjugating the indigenous people and creating a well-regulated and peaceful society. According to this view, the Aryan invaders took the first two or three castes to themselves. This view of caste, however, calls for careful reexamination. Ancient India, aside from the Aryan invasion, knew social distinctions and probably featured some form of class or caste distinction. In early times different groups were associated with different colors, the priests and teachers with white, the warriors with red, the skilled laborers with yellow, and the serfs with black.

In actual fact, there is some doubt as to whether the fourfold system of special organization ever existed in a pure form. Historically and now, there have been many more than four castes. At present there are thousands of castes or subcastes. They tend to be a group of families whose members are permitted to marry each other and who can associate with each other, especially in eating, without becoming polluted or losing their caste status. Today caste is not the fundamental social unit, as it has been described theoretically; rather the subcaste is the normal unit of association. The connotation of *varna* no longer holds, since there are dark-skinned members of the highest subcastes and light-skinned members of the lowest. Even outcastes have characteristic pride in their differences of skin color. Nor can caste or subcaste be thought of as stable or fixed. Two tendencies seem to be apparent. Some seek to combine with others to form new castes, while others, for one reason or another, tend to divide into even more exclusive subunits. Castes have also been known to rise and fall in the social scale on the basis of their own efforts.

Each caste or subcaste regulates its own affairs through a council. Such councils appear to be less prevalent and powerful in the higher castes, whereas lower caste councils are commonly quite efficient both in defining appropriate rules and customs and in enforcing them. The ultimate instrument of enforcement is expulsion from the caste. This may take place when an individual pollutes himself by violating the prescriptions of caste and fails to undertake the rituals by which his pollution will be overcome. Expulsion from caste is the ultimate fear for the devout Hindu. His *karma* requires that he remain in the caste. To violate the injunctions of caste means flying in the face of cosmic as well as social reality.

Outcastes are theoretically not permitted to take part in the caste system, but they also are recognized to some extent by Hindu society. Historically they have had to suffer greatly because of their lack of acceptance within the system. The constitution of the Republic of India, however, has granted them all the legal rights of other citizens of India, although social practice today is a far cry from constitutional prerogatives. But the outcastes in their turn maintain a kind of caste system among themselves. They are divided into various smaller groups which also are bound by restrictions on marriage and social relations.

Various anticaste movements, as mentioned earlier, have appeared in Hindu history. Those that have stressed the primacy of philosophic reasoning, as illustrated by the Upanishads, have tended to place themselves above caste restrictions. Similarly a quite liberal position toward caste has been taken by those who emphasized the importance of devotion (*bhakti*) as the means to emancipation (*moksha*). Modern reformers of Hinduism, moreover, have regularly spoken out against restrictive caste. Like their predecessors, they say that the caste system as it is now known is not an integral part of Hinduism as expressed in its sacred scriptures.

The system of caste is currently undergoing a period of serious breakdown. Several factors contribute to the situation. There is a loss of belief in the custom, even among those of the highest castes, due to democratizing influences in Indian life. Such loss of belief is bound to soften the stringencies attached to the system. Moreover, the very complexity of such a social system tends at certain points to become onerous and inefficient. Where life within the Indian villages is modified on economic grounds, the caste system seems to be viewed as a barrier to the production of desired wealth. Political movements within India, especially those among the outcastes, have tended to view caste as a block to representation and full personal usefulness in the society. The government of post-partition

India has placed itself squarely against much if not all of the traditional meaning of caste. As the younger generation in India becomes Westernized, educationally and socially, the caste system is viewed as archaic, expendable, and unjust. And the trend toward urbanization is also a strong factor in lessening its barriers. Yet while caste today is weakened, it does exist. It may ultimately pass away, but that time is still far off.

Hinduism is the world's oldest religion. It has undergone many changes in the past. Today its redefinition and renewal probably indicate that it will be a vital force in the lives of countless Indians for a long time into the future.

ANNOTATED BIBLIOGRAPHY
ON HINDUISM

1 BOUQUET, ALAN. *Hinduism.* New York: Longmans, Green & Co., 1950. A good, basic source.

*2 DEUSSEN, PAUL, translator. *The Philosophy of the Upanishads.* New York: Dover Press, 1966. The title describes the contents.

*3 FISCHER, LOUIS. *Gandhi: His Life and Message for the World* New York: Mentor Books, New American Library, 1954. The story of the Indian leader who led India's struggle for freedom and who taught and exemplified the teaching of nonviolence.

4 HUTTON, J. H. *Caste in India: Its Nature, Function, and Origins,* 3d. ed. New York: Oxford University Press, 1961. A comprehensive description from a long-term member of the Indian Civil Service.

*5 ISHERWOOD, CHRISTOPHER, ed. and intro. *Vedanta for Modern Man.* New York: Collier Books, 1962. Sixty-one essays on various phases of the philosophy and technique of Vedanta.

6 MACNICOL, N., ed. *Hindu Scriptures.* New York: E. P. Dutton & Co., 1938. Hymns from the *Rig Veda,* five *Upanishads,* and the *Bhagavad Gita.*

7 MAHADEVAN, T. M. P. *Outlines of Hinduism.* Bombay: Chetana Limited, 1956. A valuable introduction to the study of Hinduism in its religious, philosophical, and ethical aspects.

8 MORGAN, KENNETH, ed. *The Religion of the Hindus.* New York: Ronald Press, 1953. A comprehensive account of the nature, history, beliefs, and practices of Hinduism by practitioners of the faith.

9 NIKHILANANDA, SWAMI. *Hinduism: Its Meaning for the Liberation of the Spirit.* New York: Harper & Brothers, 1958. A survey of Hindu beliefs and customs.

*10 PITT, MALCOLM. *Introducing Hinduism.* New York: Friendship Press, 1955. A sixty-page introduction to a complex subject.

* Paperback.

*11 RADHAKRISHNAN, SARVEPALLI. *Eastern Religions and Western Thought.* New York: Oxford University Press, 1959. Wise lectures on Hinduism and related matters.

12 RADHAKRISHNAN, SARVEPALLI. *The Hindu View of Life.* New York: The Macmillan Co., 1962. A learned philosopher outlines the system of underlying beliefs that have guided ordinary Indian families for many centuries.

13 RENOU, LOUIS. *Hinduism.* New York: George Braziller, 1961. One book in a series on the great religions of modern man.

*14 SEN, KSHITA. *Hinduism.* Baltimore: Penguin Books, 1961. An exposition of the nature and historical development of Hinduism, with extracts from the Hindu scriptures.

15 WHEELER, MORTIMER. *Civilization of the Indus Valley and Beyond.* New York: McGraw-Hill Book Co., 1966. A recent account of Indian antiquity.

*16 WOOD, ERNEST. *Yoga.* Baltimore: Penguin Books, 1959. An explanation of the philosophy and practices of Indian *yoga* and how it can be applied to the West today.

*17 ZINKIN, TAYA. *Caste Today.* New York: Oxford University Press, 1962. Briefly describes the caste system in India today.

Jainism

A GLOSSARY OF JAIN TERMS

Acharya	The religious head of the Terapanthis order in Jainism.
Adharma	The principle of rest as opposed to *dharma*, the principle of motion.
Agamas	One of the chief scriptures of Jainism, meaning "precepts."
Ahimsa	Noninjury, harmlessness, or nonviolence.
Ajiva	The nonsoul or nonself.
Akasa	Space.
Amanaska	Those living beings that do not possess a mind.
Angas	The name for the twelve sections of the Agamas.
Aparigraha	Nonattachment to wordly things.
Arjikas	Female ascetics.
Asrava	The influx of karmic matter into the soul.
Asteya	Abstinence from stealing.
Atman	Self or soul.
Avipaka nirjara	Inducing karmic matter to leave the soul through ascetic exercises.
Bandha	The bondage of the soul by karmic matter.
Brahmacharya	Freedom from unchastity and all sexual pleasures.
Dharma	A duty or social reality, an essential quality, or the medium of motion.
Digambaras	A major Jain sect, who believe it not proper to wear clothing: the "sky-clad."
Jain	A follower of the Jina, an honorific title for Mahavira.
Jiva	The soul or self.
Kala	Time.
Karma	The principle of causality in moral experience.
Mahavira	The title of the founder of Jainism, meaning victor, conqueror, great man, or hero.
Moksha	Ultimate release of salvation.

83

Mukta	The liberated soul.
Munis	Male ascetics.
Nirjara	The gradual removal of karmic matter from the soul.
Nirvana	Enlightenment, freedom from self, the end of selfish desires, the state of salvation.
Pudgala	Materiality.
Raja	King, chief, or ruler.
Ratnatraya	The three jewels of right belief, right knowledge, and right conduct.
Sadhus	Male ascetics.
Sadhvis	Female ascetics.
Sakala	Perfect or unqualified conduct.
Samanaska	Those living beings who possess a mind.
Samsarin	The embodied souls of living beings.
Samvara	Stopping the influx of karmic matter into the soul.
Samyag-darsana	Right belief.
Samyag-jnana	Right knowledge.
Samyak-charitra	Right conduct.
Sangha	The religious order in Jainism.
Satya	Freedom from falsehood; truth.
Savipaka nirjara	The matured state of *karma*.
Shvetambaras	A major Jain sect, who believed it proper to wear clothing, the "white-clad."
Siddha	The liberated soul.
Siddhantas	One of the chief scriptures of Jainism, meaning "treatises."
Sravakas	Male laity.
Sravikas	Female laity.
Sthanakavasis	A major Jain subsect, who reject idol worship.
Sthavara	Immobile or one-sensed souls.
Stupa	Originally a burial mound; later, elaborate structures, also known as pagodas.
Sutra	A text spoken by Mahavira himself.
Tattvas	Seven propositions basic to salvation.
Terapanthis	A major Jain subsect, who are organized under a religious head.

Tirthankaras	Twenty-four predecessors of the inception of Jainism, meaning "those who guide the people to gain liberation."
Trasa	Mobile or many-sensed souls.
Vikala	Imperfect or qualified conduct.
Yatis	Male ascetics.
Yoga	The method and practice leading to union of the self with the divine.

III

JAINISM

INTRODUCTION

HINDUISM GAVE BIRTH to three religions: Jainism, Buddhism, and Sikhism. Jainism was its first offspring, and like any child it appears in a certain light to be somewhat like its mother. Yet, as will be seen, there are signs that this faith is indeed uniquely itself.

Jainism is an example of a heresy becoming an independent religion. Mahavira (599-527 B.C.), its nominal founder, was essentially a reformer. He did not reject the Hinduism into which he had been born, nor was he rejected by Hinduism. His efforts were primarily directed toward the establishment within Hinduism of cetain teachings which he and his small body of sympathetic contemporaries thought to be essential Hinduism. He did oppose certain tendencies in Hinduism, and spoke so clearly for a select number of others that in time the resulting corpus of teaching, cultic practice, and congregational organization became an independent religion.

Jainism may be paired with Buddhism, discussed in the next chapter, as a revolt against particular features of Hinduism. Hinduism in India and elsewhere is orthodoxy; Jainism and Buddhism are heterodoxy. Jainism and Buddhism originated as separate religions only in relation to Hinduism. They did not create absolutely new expressions of man's relations to nature, his fellow man, and to the divine. They are part and parcel of a particular cultural stream. Yet, insofar as they selected points within Hinduism for emphasis, they can be understood only on their own terms.

Hinduism is a remarkably flexible, tolerant, and absorptive religion. Over the centuries it has been able to maintain within itself

86

the highest degree of diversity. It is perhaps as difficult to be a genuine heretic within Hinduism as in any other religion found in advanced societies. But for a period of about a thousand years, Buddhism made great headway in India. A leading Buddhist ruler, Asoka (d. 226 B.C.?), encouraged Buddhism throughout the length and breadth of the land. Indeed, in his time a local prophet might have said that Hinduism probably would die out. But Hinduism was enormously resilient. It lived to see the day when Buddhism waned in India, and in fact left the subcontinent for greener pastures. While Buddhism flourishes elsewhere in Asia, its defeat by Hinduism in India has been for centuries an accomplished fact.

But not so Jainism. Jainism, like Buddhism, became an independent religion. It succeeded centuries ago in attracting many Indians, and grew up and established itself as a separate religious force in Indian life. Its triumph was not as great as that of Buddhism, but it was widespread. When the time came for Hinduism to display its perennial vitality and absorptive powers, Jainism did not disappear. It did not go elsewhere. It stood its ground, although greatly reduced in the number of its adherents. Jainism continues today as an important factor in the life of India and at least one province of Pakistan.

Hinduism, like a wide flowing river, has picked up silt and pebbles from a broad terrain. It absorbed the key emphases of both Jainism and Buddhism, although in a sense it already displayed them before these religions began. One of the several elements taken into Hinduism from Jainism was a stress upon the individuality of persons and their worth. Jainism also contributed a kindly attitude; its valuing of all living beings tended to curb certain excesses in Vedic and Brahmanic Hinduism.

Originally Jainism did not intend to be a numerically or geographically limited religion. Three passages in two of the canonical scriptures record that Mahavira believed himself to be responsible for the propagation of a religion that would be universal. But the dream was never implemented. This is a nonmissionary religion which has always been limited to this part of Asia, and its membership has been slowly declining for several centuries.

The current Jain community is spread all over India and parts of Pakistan—from Kashmir to Travancore and from Sind to Bengal. More than 40 per cent of its adherents, however, are found in Bombay Province and Bihar, including Baroda. Nearly 25 per cent live in Rajputana and Ajmer-Merwara, about 8 per cent in the Central India Agency, and 7 per cent in the United Provinces. The remainder are scattered over the other parts of the subcontinent and are most numerous in the Central Provinces and Berar, the Punjab, Mysore, Madras, Hyderabad, and Delhi. Thus, in the main, Jainism is currently strongest in western India.

According to the 1951 census in India proper there were at that time 1,618,406 Jains. This number indicates that the Jain population itself has increased since the first census in 1881 placed its number at 1,221,896. But the proportion of Jains in the total population of India has declined between 1881 and 1951. In 1881 the proportion to the total population of India was .48 per cent and in 1951 it was .45 per cent—in any case less than one half of 1 per cent. Of course, all statistics regarding religion as well as many other matters need to be accepted with considerable caution.

A number of factors account for the present decline in the number of Jains. First, the birth rate is low. In this connection it is important to note that the sex composition of the Jains is not even. The 1941 census showed that there were only 930 Jain females for every 1,000 Jain males. A deficiency of females is greater for Jains than for any other group in India, such as Hindus, Christians, or Jews. This deficiency has been continuous through the past decades. Although endogamy is not a strict requirement, it is a factor. There is some evidence to show that the fertility of Jain women is less than that of other groups in India. Similarly the practice of child marriage, found to a major extent among Jains, has negatively influenced the number of births. Jains also tend to concentrate in urban areas, where the birth rate is notably low.

Second, the strength of the Jains has been undermined by various religious divisions within the community. They are split into two or three major sects and hundreds of subsects. Each has tended to magnify its own separateness. In consequence Jains have spent considerable energy in rationalizing and defending their divisions, which make marriages between the members belonging to different sects and subsects extremely difficult. In addition, caste distinctions carried over from Hinduism exacerbate the separateness. For these and other reasons Jainism is not holding its own in India.

The followers of Mahavira call themselves "Jains" or "Jaina." This term signifies that they are followers of the Jina, an honorific title traditionally given to Mahavira. It means conqueror or victor. Thus the Jain is a follower of the Victorious One.

FOUNDER

Jainism is the oldest personally founded religion in India. Unlike Hinduism it looks to a person as its initiator and leader. Although the founder of a religion combines a number of charismatic elements in his leadership, he may be differentiated from other kinds of religious leaders, such as the prophet, the reformer, the saint, and the priest. Others may be impressed with a sense of their calling, but the founder is characterized by an even more intense and grandiloquent conception of his mission, to which his own response is considered to be in every way mandatory and divine. Mahavira, the founder of Jainism, meets all the requirements of the founder of a religion.

The dates of his life are somewhat uncertain. Usually he is said to have been born in 599 B.C. and died in 527. He established Jainism during a period which was religiously and philosophically of great creative importance, alike for India and for other parts of the world. In India he was a contemporary of Buddha, so that two religions of lasting significance were born in one region at practically the same time. In addition, and also about that time, Confucius and Lao-Tze were founding their religions in China, and Zoroaster was finding success with his teachings in what is now Iran. Judaism, too, was then under the influence of its great prophets: Jeremiah, Ezekiel, and the Isaiah of the Exile. In Greece, philosophy experienced major development through such philosophers as Anaximander, Anaximenes, Heraclitus, Pythagoras, Thales, and Xenophanes. All overlapped the life of Mahavira.

The Jains claim that their religion originated in hoary antiquity. According to their view, there were twenty-four Tirthankaras, those who guided the people to attain liberation. These slowly built up the Jain heritage which Mahavira capped with his own life and teachings as the twenty-fourth of the series. No historical evidence has been found, however, to prove beyond doubt even the existence of the first twenty-two. The last two, Parshva and Mahavira, have been shown to be historical personages.

Some scholars believe that the heritage was created in a different way. They say that Mahavira was indeed the founder of Jainism and did become acquainted with a group of ascetics who lived by the teachings of Parshva. But the idea of the Tirthankaras arose, they say, after Jainism was established, and was a device by which its adherents sought to formulate a respectable religious tradition. In this matter, as in so many others connected with the four religions of Asia, the blending of fact with legend is a complicated and important problem on which scholars are currently working.

Parshva lived and taught about 250 years before Mahavira, that is, toward the end of the ninth century B.C. His teachings were opposed to the then dominant culture of the Brahmanas. He was against the caste system and advocated the egalitarian inclusion of all persons within his religious community without distinction of caste, creed, or sex. He strongly opposed the killing of animals in Vedic sacrifices, which in the Brahmanic period were a dominant feature of Hinduism. He preached the four great vows: noninjury (*ahimsa*), truth (*satya*), abstinence from stealing (*asteya*), and nonattachment to worldly things (*aparigraha*). Parshva's teachings emphasized the necessity of strict asceticism as the instrument for attainment of release (*moksha*). He also divided his followers into four categories according to sex and the strictness with which the members were obligated to practice the teachings: male ascetics (*yatis, sadhus,* or *munis*), female ascetics (*arjikas* or *sadhvis*), male laity (*sravakas*), and female laity (*sravikas*). These four orders in the religious community were led by members who supervised their conduct. Thus Parshva, as a real person and aside from the entire

tradition which was mainly mythic, laid the basis upon which
Mahavira built the religion of Jainism.

Mahavira was born in Kundadrama, a suburb of the flourishing
city of Vaisali in the northeastern province of Bihar. Growing up
far from the natural center of Vedic and Brahamanic Hinduism,
he was perhaps less dependent upon the Hindu past. He was of
non-Aryan stock and was not related to Brahman ancestors, upon
whom orthodox Vedic traditions depended. He was a Kshatriya of
the Jnata clan. His religion—interestingly, like that of the Buddha
—did not evolve from a priestly or intellectual family tradition. This
teacher of nonviolence was born and raised, paradoxically, in a
Kshatriya or warrior household, although his parents, Siddhartha
and Trisala, were probably inclined toward pacifism.

Mahavira is the name by which the founder of Jainism is commonly known. This term, however, is an honorific title meaning
Great Man or Hero. His original name was Nataputta Vardhamana.
His father was a raja, according to tradition, who typically surrounded his children with the available luxuries of the time. In
early life he was attended by five nurses and indulged in the
pleasures of sense. In due course he married and had a daughter,
Anojja. Yasoda was his wife's name. In his thirtieth year his parents
died and his elder brother, Nandivardhana, took over the direction
of the palace.

Prior to these events, Mahavira had come upon a body of monks
who followed the rule of Parshva. They lived in a district outside
of the town and were readily accessible to him. Upon the death of
his parents and the ascent to power of his brother, Mahavira asked
the latter's consent to his own abandonment of the princely life. His
brother agreed, on condition that Mahavira should remain in the
palace for one more year, during which he could give up his possessions systematically and prepare himself for the monastic existence.

When the time came he retired from the world, joining the
monks outside the town in a cell. By the terms of the initiation
ceremony he discarded all his possessions except one white robe.
According to tradition, he plucked out the hair of his head in five

handfuls. He also took a pledge to neglect his body and suffer all calamities that might befall him. Thirteen months later he discarded his robe and thenceforth went about completely naked in his wanderings through the villages of India. If possible, he never remained more than one night in a village or for more than five nights in a town. He was firm in his rejection of any attachment to people or places that might bind him to sensual satisfactions. Gradually he gave up being a solitary ascetic, assuming the leadership of many monks. His teachings apparently were relatively simple and severe. He declared that no one can save his own soul without, among other requirements, practicing the strictest asceticism. He also taught that this asceticism requires the practice of harmlessness (ahimsa) toward any and all living forms. Although neither of these teachings originated with Mahavira, nor indeed with his predecessor, Parshva, it was the genius of Mahavira to combine them with clarity and force, and in addition to exemplify them in his daily life.

He took great pains not to injure any living being. When walking he carried a soft broom for sweeping the path, since it might have on it tiny living things. He examined his bed on retiring to make sure that he would not crush anything that lived. He did not eat raw food, but rather food prepared originally for someone else and left over. Before drinking water he would strain it with a cloth. For twelve years he sought deliverance (moksha), wandering about in India and giving himself only to the austerities of severe self-denial. At last, during the thirteenth year, outside the town of Grimbhika-grama, on the northern bank of the River Rigupalika in the field of the householder Samaga, "facing in a northeasterly direction from an old temple not far from a sal tree," and squatting with knees high and head low in the attitude of deep meditation, he reached nirvana. He had achieved the state of the Jina, the Victor, and thus it became known to his followers that victory over the constraints of the flesh was truly possible.

Upon reaching the state of nirvana, Mahavira began most actively to promulgate his faith. He felt he possessed a mission to inform everyone of the possibility of such an attainment. He was persuasive, and conversions in considerable numbers followed. Then for thirty years he organized his followers on the basis of his beliefs and experiences. At the age of seventy-two he died. He is no longer subject to rebirth, according to Jain doctrine, but blissfully exists in a place of reward called Isatpragbhara. As the twenty-fourth Tirthankara or Crossing-Maker, Mahavira by his own crossing of the bridge between time and eternity, and his subsequent teaching and organizing on the basis of his experience, gave to the world the new religion of Jainism.

Mahavira is not remembered primarily for his intellectual profundity. He was not essentially a philosopher or theologian. He expounded his ideas with severe clarity and intensity, but his teachings do not equal in depth those, for example, of the Upanishadic writers. Again, he was not primarily a social reformer. His teachings did have implications for personal and social living, but it was not his aim to create social unrest or a doctrinaire program of social amelioration. There were, in fact, significant social consequences, but these results were not at the forefront of Mahavira's intentions. Rather, his life was characterized by a deep personal striving for salvation. The path he sought was for himself; that it was also a path by which others could travel to the blessed state was a derivative gain. Thus Jainism for Mahavira, as it has been for countless others, was basically a highly individualized effort to overcome the negativities of the world of karmic existence.

As is true of the founders of other religions, Mahavira believed that no object exists that should be worshiped. Yet he himself became an object of supreme veneration in later times. The scriptures of Jainism attribute divine characteristics to him. They claim that he was the incarnate form of the divine and that he existed before his incarnation. They say also that he was sinless and omniscient. Jain temples today display statues of Mahavira, similar to the idols of other faiths, making his deification concrete.

HISTORY

During the lifetime of Mahavira, Jainism was geographically limited. His followers lived mainly where he taught: in Bihar,

Orissa, and West Bengal. But after his death his disciples succeeded in extending the faith throughout much of India. During this time, Jainism received the support of kings as well as of plain people.

The very scatteredness of rising Jainism probably made it difficult for the leaders of the movement to supervise their followers. In different parts of the subcontinent diverse customs, manners, and ways of life entered into the practices of the new religion. These variations may well be related to the factionalism that emerged later.

During these early years the teachings of Mahavira were not committed to writing, but were carried forward by oral tradition. As is known elsewhere, oral tradition is readily open to corruption, despite the fact that at times it is fantastically accurate. And it was not until the Council of Pataliputra in the early part of the third century B.C. that the scriptures of the religion were canonized.

In the early period, a renewed emphasis was placed upon the importance of the twenty-three Tirthankaras who were thought to have preceded Mahavira. Thus Parshva, who immediately preceded him, had a temple built to his honor on Mt. Parasnath, some two hundred miles northwest of Calcutta. To Nemi, the twenty-second Tirthankara, a temple was erected upon the cliff under Mt. Girnar in far-western India. Other Tirthankaras were similarly honored.

Jainism was favored on many occasions by political leaders in India. It first received the appreciation of rajas in east India. It is said that Chetaka, the most eminent among the Lichchavi princes and the ruler of Vaisali, was in late life a noteworthy patron of Jainism. He was, of course, an uncle of Mahavira, having earlier given his sister, Princess Trisala, in marriage to Siddhartha, Mahavira's father. The Nandas (413-322 B.C., rulers of what is modern Bihare), are reputed to have been Jains, since an inscription of the period shows King Nanda I leading a conquering expedition into Kalinga to carry off an image of Adi-Jina. Tradition also has it that Chandragupta Maurya was a Jain and that he left his throne to join the Jain migration to the south of India, dying in the faith twelve years later. Some say that the famous edicts of Asoka reveal Jainism as his faith before his conversion to Buddhism. Certainly it seems clear that he was at least tolerant of it, since he donated five monastery caves to the Jains, "for so long as the sun and moon do endure." Samprati, grandson and successor of Asoka, also was at least sympathetic with Jainism and established Jain temples and monasteries.

Other rulers in eastern India throughout the various centuries likewise gave support to the thriving religion. What was true here, moreover, was also characteristic of other regions, including north India where Hinduism was strongest. At times, on the other hand, Jainism met with resistance and disaster, as in the period of Muslim prominence; although a notable exception in that era was the liberal-minded Akbar.

In the course of its history Jainism has contributed heavily to the art and architecture of the region. The Jains, however, were not original in their form; they adopted the building traditions of the locality in which they found themselves. In north India, for example, they followed the Vaishnava in building, while in south India they adhered to the Dravidian type. The form of their *stupas* is barely distinguishable from that of the Buddhists, and their elaborately curved steeples are identical in outline with those of the Brahmanical temples. But while Jain style is not distinctive, it does express itself in some of the finest specimens of local architecture. Jains have a great love of attractive natural settings, where they build *stupas*, temples, cave-temples, pillars, and towers which are esthetically valuable for their elaborate detail and exquisite finish. Such show places, usually the gift of wealthy Jains, are found practically everywhere in India and in parts of Pakistan. In other art forms, such as decorative sculpture, the Jains also excel.

Historically, Jainism has made a significant contribution to mysticism. In its beginnings it was a relatively simple faith. It abjured extensive ceremony and social differentiation. Later, however, it grew in complexity. The priesthood became an important force in formalizing the religion and ceremonialism, including image worship became widespread. In the fourteenth and fifteenth centuries A.D., however, a number of movements arose as a reaction which aimed at restoration of the original and simple faith. These movements found strength in mysticism, and Tara Swami and Lunka Shah are noteworthy names in this renewal. Ramamuni's poem *Pahuda Doha* represents an important form of this mysticism.

Sectarianism has been one of the principal features of Jainism. Historically and at present, as we have seen, it is divided into a number of subgroups of greater and lesser importance. Two of the most significant derive from relatively early times: the Shvetambaras and the Digambaras. The Shvetambaras (the "white-clad") found it proper to wear at least one garment. The Digambaras, on the other hand, won their name by being "clad in atmosphere." The name also means "air-dressed" or "sky-clad." Because Mahavira went naked, this latter group did without clothing. The Shvetambaras, however, lived mainly in the north, where they were affected by the cold winds and cultural influences of the region. The doctrine of the Digambaras was more suitable to the warmth of south India. The two groups split apart about the year 82 A.D.

The Shvetambaras readily admit women to their monastic order, and assume that women have the same chance to enter *nirvana* as men. The Digambaras, however, take their stand on what they claim was Mahavira's view of woman as the greatest temptation in the world and the cause of all sinful acts. According to this group, therefore, the only way women can be delivered from earthly evil (*moksha*) is to be reborn as men.

The two sects have other differences. The Digambaras, for example, believe that once a person has attained *nirvana* he has no need of food, but is able to sustain life without eating. The Shvetambaras disagree. The Digambaras also believe that the ancient scriptures of Jainism have completely disappeared and are unavailable for current guidance. The Shvetambaras believe in the canonical books. Digambaras assert that Mahavira never married, while the Shvetambaras believe he not only married but had a daughter. Digambaras say that Jain idols should be nude, as are the true followers; Shvetambaras cover their idols in white cloth, as they themselves are clad. Each of these sects is divided into many subsects.

In more recent times two other Jain sects have come into being. One, the Sthanakavasis, arose about 1650 A.D., possibly under the influence of the Islam abhorrence of idols. It grew up in Ahmedabad, the city of Gujerat which was at the time under strongly Islamic influence. Sthanakavasis do not believe in idol worship. They cover their mouths with strips of white cloth in order to prevent the inhalation of flying and even microscopic creatures, the cloth being a symbol of purity.

Another nonidolatrous sect, that of Terapanthis, was founded by Swami Bhikkhanaji Maharaja in 1817 A.D. He broke from the Sthanakavasis because of differences in other doctrines and practices. The Terapanthis sect requires very severe penance of its sinners. It also teaches a highly systematized set of doctrines, has a notable organization under a religious head (acharya), and holds a festival once a year in which all members gather together for a discussion of the problems of the sect.

Sectarianism comprises a most important problem to the whole of Jainism. It is not possible to speak of this religion sociologically as a single unity. Its diversity of form, as mentioned earlier, prevents it from being a conspicuously strong force in the life of modern India or elsewhere. Yet the ideas of the various sectarian groups have had their influence far beyond the membership. Gandhi, for example, who lived near Bombay, currently a center of Jainism, was attracted to the religion as well as to Buddhist ideas during a short period of personal rebellion against Hinduism. Quite possibly his intense stress on nonviolence (ahimsa) may have been influenced by Jainism.

SCRIPTURES

The Jains, unlike the Muslims, Sikhs, and other religious groups of India and Pakistan do not have a language of their own. They use the language of the region. Far from having merely assumed the regional languages of the subcontinent, however, they have contributed in notable manner to their enrichment.

Mahavira taught in the Ardhamagadhi language of his own region, and as a consequence a number of the sacred scriptures of Jainism are written in that language. Jain scholars today must learn

Mahavira's language in order to understand their sacred records. Some of the later scriptures were written in Sanskrit; therefore, scholarly Jains must learn it as well.

In southern India the history of Jainism has been bound to the development of the Kanada language in evident ways. Names of Jain writers such as Pampa, Ponna, and Ranna are inextricably interwoven with the best of Kanada literature. During the reign of the Gangas in that region, Jain-inspired literature received considerable stimulation through political patronage. And Jainism has similarly contributed to other vernaculars, such as Prakrit and Apabhramsa.

A great part of the Jain literature has been preserved. It exists in large part, however, only in manuscript form, for few of the scriptues have been published. They treat of mathematics, medicine, astrology, grammar, vocabulary, prosody, and other topics, using various literary forms: poetry, prose, story, *sutra*, etc. It is to be hoped that before too long an extensive historical and literary analysis of the extant literature of Jainism will throw great light upon that religion.

The Jains, however, are not strongly attached to their sacred scriptures and do not look upon them in general as literally inspired. Usually they content themselves with reciting only the names of their books. Of these the Agamas (precepts) or Siddhantas (treatises) are the chief. (Although the Agamas are canonically divided into twelve sections, or *Angas*, the twelfth has been lost.)

The various sects within Jainism recognize different numbers of documents as canonical. The Shvetambaras sect, for example, recognizes forty-five, while the Sthanakavasis recognize only thirty-three. Other sectarian groups acknowledge the authority of more or fewer documents.

TEACHINGS

The teachings of Jainism can be understood only in relationship to Hinduism, which is the doctrinal, cultic, and communal soil out of which Jainism grew. Practically all its teachings can be found in one form or another within the Hinduism that preceded Mahavira. This teacher originated a religion, but did not put forth essentially new truths. His teachings are in large measure a reaction or response to certain features of Hinduism which gave him cause for uneasiness. Of these, six may be mentioned briefly.

1. The doctrine of *karma*, the law of causation as applied to the moral sphere, seemed to him too rigid and restrictive, for within Hinduism its rule is absolute. He sought to lessen this rigidity and to find a practical measure of release from it.

2. The Hindu conception of rebirth came to mean, especially in the Upanishadic period, that individual souls do not possess real individuality. According to Hindu doctrine souls do not remain individualized in eternity, but become absorbed in Brahma. Mahavira strongly asserted the independence or autonomy of the individual soul.

3. Hinduism taught caste. In Mahavira's time these lines of social organization were still in the making, and he benefited to a considerable extent personally from the system. But he was strongly democratic, believing in the worth of all individuals. He taught the importance of a casteless society.

4. The priestly caste, as a result of the solidifying caste system, was clearly becoming the most influential group in Indian life. Mahavira was a member of the second or warrior caste. This had much to lose as the priesthood became dominant in the society, and a good deal of the impact of early Jainism was in opposition to the prominence of the priestly caste.

5. Particularly in the Vedic and Brahmanic periods, Hinduism was polytheistic. One hymn in the Vedic literature suggests that the gods may number as many as 3,333. Mahavira, in the simplicity of his character, was repelled by the extremes of Vedic polytheism. In fact, he did not teach the existence of a god at all.

6. Hinduism in the Vedic and Brahmanic period also taught the importance of animal sacrifices. These ceremonial occasions became complex affairs with large numbers of animals slaughtered. Mahavira may well have developed his emphasis upon harmlessness (*ahimsa*) to all living things in response to the excesses of animal sacrifice in his time.

Yet his precepts were not an outright denial of the teachings of

Hinduism. *Karma* and rebirth, for example, were retained in modified form by Mahavira, as were other doctrines derived from the Hinduism of his time.

The teachings of Jainism are not philosophically developed or influential. Compared to the elaborate philosophical systems of Hinduism and Buddhism, it cannot claim distinction as a system of thought. From one point of view, it may be considered a religious or theological middle ground between Hinduism and Buddhism, both of which are highly developed. Jainism, on the contrary, is essentially a system of quiet contemplation and asceticism. Jains are persons who are free from any sort of attachment to the world because they have attained supreme knowledge and have subjugated their passions. It is a religion not essentially based upon the incarnation of a deity or a sacred book of nonhuman origin.

In brief, Jainism is based upon four fundamental principles. First, man's personality is dual: material and spiritual. Second, he is not perfect because of the existence of *karma* in his soul. Third, by his spiritual nature he can and must control his material nature. Fourth, the separation of an individual soul from the obstructing matter combined with it is the responsibility solely of the individual himself, by his own efforts. These four principles undergird the whole of Jainism.

God

Original Jainism had no teachings regarding the existence of God, whether deity be conceived as personal, transpersonal, or impersonal. Mahavira rejected the polytheistic beliefs of Vedic and Brahmanic Hinduism, a rejection apparently based on the conviction that the gods are superfluous. In fact, early Jainism at least implied that belief in God is incompatible with self-responsibiilty—a cardinal virtue in this mode of thought. Mahavira in this spirit scolded those who prayed to a deity or even discussed the subject. Praying, to Mahavira, represented an attitude of dependence upon God. He opposed all attachments, divine as well as human. If it were claimed that God is a helpful friend, Mahavira answered that man is his own friend and should not seek a friend beyond himself.

This teacher, moreover, did not take kindly to the cosmological argument for the existence of God. To those who claimed that the universe must necessarily depend upon a creative force, Mahavira answered that they did not know the truth. Apparently he was in accord with certain strands of Hindu thought which assume that the universe is eternal and therefore not in need of creation. At any rate, he was not a believer in a Supreme Being. Because of this negative attitude, one can scarcely consider him a theologian. Indeed, he systematically avoided most of the chief topics of concern to theologians.

He did not, however, develop an intellectually detailed system of thought. His philosophy, such as it is, may be seen in part as a reaction to the monistic idealism of the Hindu philosophers. These teachers, as was evident in the growing literature called the Upanishads, taught the unreality of the body and the external world. They stressed the essential self (*atman*), and the transpersonal deity, Brahma, as the only true realities. Such a view was congenial to many Hindus, but Mahavira judged it inadequate. He found that he could not deny the reality of external things and of the body. Both these types of existence seemed very real to him. In fact he seemed to feel the burden of them keenly. Finally, finding belief in Brahma or a similar deity unnecessary, Mahavira asserted that the whole universe can be divided into two categories: the soul (*jiva*) and the nonsoul (*ajiva*). These two elements between them exhaust all that exists in the universe. All that is has resulted from the interaction of these two elements. By their interaction they create certain energies which bring about birth and the multifarious experiences of life and death. The spiritual task of the individual consists in overcoming this interaction. By disciplining the material existence and securing mastery over it, the spiritual existence becomes supreme. Thus salvation (*moksha*) is possible, though its attainment is arduous.

The whole process of salvation in Jainism has been given classic formulation as consisting of seven propositions or realities (*tattvas*): (1) living substance (*jiva*), (2) matter or nonliving substance (*ajiva*), (3) the influx of karmic matter into the soul (*asrava*), (4) the bondage of the soul by karmic matter (*bandha*), (5) the stopping of *asrava* (*samvara*), (6) the gradual removal of karmic matter (*nirjara*), and (7) the attainment of perfect freedom (*moksha*). Obviously the first two of the *tattvas* are concerned with the enumeration and nature of the eternal substances of reality. The last five are concerned with the interaction between them: the steps leading to deliverance from the conflict between the first two.

Since the *tattvas* comprise the basic ingredients of Jain philosophy and are required learning for believers, brief comments on them are in order. The first principle, *jiva*, is the most important. It indicates that the whole world is filled with an infinite number of souls. These beings are substances. Their primary characteristic is intelligence. They can never be destroyed; they are eternal. Although the unimpeded soul is absolutely perfect and powerful, it identifies itself through ignorance with matter. This indentification leads to its degradation and the variety of evils that characterize human life.

The soul may be described as having two aspects. One is the mundane soul (*samsarin*). Mundane souls are the embodied souls of living beings in the world and are subject to rebirth. The second aspect is the liberated soul (*siddha* or *mukta*). Liberated souls are not embodied. They exist in absolute purity and perfection at the top of the universe. They are unconcerned with worldly affairs. Having reached *nirvana* they are able to experience four joys: unlimited perception, perfect knowledge, infinite power, and unbounded happiness. A relatively simple though metaphysically profound difference exists between the mundane and the liberated aspects of the soul. The former is permeated with subtle matter. The latter is completely pure and free from any material contamination.

A number of conditions characterize the mundane aspect of the soul. As it has lived in the past and is living now, so shall it live forever. While it possesses perception and knowledge, it is immaterial, that is, does not have touch, taste, smell, or color. It only is responsible for all its actions, and necessarily experiences their consequences; it completely fills the material body which it occupies, whether that of a fly or an elephant. Despite the fact that it wanders in the state of the mundane, it possesses the possibility of becoming perfect (*siddha*) because it has the tendency to seek its liberated aspect (*mukta*).

Jains have tried philosophically to classify the mundane or embodied souls according to categories of complexity and worth. One effort distinguishes between those living beings who have a mind (*samanaska*) and those who do not (*amanaska*). Another twofold classification speaks of the immobile or one-sensed souls (*sthavara*) and the mobile or many-sensed souls (*trasa*). The first category is further divided into five kinds of souls: earth-bodied, water-bodied, fire-bodied, air-bodied, and vegetable-bodied. The second category is divided into four classes on the basis of the number of senses involved.

Jainism's second principle, *ajiva*, consists of nonliving substances. These substances, like the living, possess several characteristics. They exist permanently, since they have not been created and cannot be destroyed. They also possess their own particular attributes and modes.

Nonliving substances are of five kinds: matter (*pudgala*), the medium of motion (*dharma*), the medium of rest (*adharma*), space (*akasa*), and time (*kala*). Some of these nonliving substances are clearly characterized by materiality—those that possess bodies and can be perceived by the sense organs. Others, such as *dharma*, *adharma*, *akasa*, and *kala* are clearly immaterial. They are nevertheless delimiting conditions of the free operation of the nonsoul.

The third principle, *asrava*, states that karmic matter has involved itself in the very constitution of the soul. The combination is evident, for example, in the thought processes of the individual person —in his speech and bodily activities. Karmic matter confuses itself with the *jiva* in such subtle ways that it is commonly not possible for the senses to perceive it.

The fourth principle, *bandha*, teaches that the karmic matter upon entering the soul places the soul in bondage to the nonsoul. The union of the soul and the nonsoul does not imply the complete obliteration of the natural properties of each, but according to the quantity and quality of karmic material absorbed, the two basic elements are restricted in their free and full functioning. The fusion of spirit and matter, therefore, creates a compound entity in which the distributing elements are continuously present. Jain philosophers have described other kinds of bondage of the soul, depending upon the nature of karmic matter, the duration of the attachment, the intensity of the bondage, and the number of karmic molecules which attach to the soul.

The fifth principle, *samvara*, signifies the process whereby matter is prevented from approaching the *jiva*. In that state of *samvara*, the individual by discipline sets up a protective wall which shuts out all of the karmic matter that seeks to become entwined with the soul. In this stage of the process toward salvation, the living entity is disciplined to become strong enough to arrest the agelong situation in which souls through wrong belief, lack of faith, nonrenunciation, carelessness, indulgence of the passions, and other kinds of lowly bondage naturally find themselves.

The sixth principle, *nirjara*, is an extension of the previous principle. *Nirjara* signifies the falling away of karmic matter from the *jiva*. As the karmic matter becomes ripe, it is capable of being cut off from the essential self. Jainism teaches that the falling away of karmic matter from the soul occurs at moments when the karmic matter is naturally matured (*savipaka nirjara*). But the karmic matter can be induced to leave the soul through ascetic practices (*avipaka nirjara*). The latter force involves the deliberate practice of austerities.

The seventh and final principle, *moksha*, involves the freeing of the spirits from all matter. In this state the soul and the nonsoul are completely separated from each other. All karmic matter has left the soul and indeed none of it ever can be combined with the soul. In this stage the soul reaches its full and unimpeded existence. The *samsarin* becomes the *siddha*. But the attainment of this stage does not mean that the existence of matter is negated. It simply implies that the free soul is no longer contaminated by whatever karmic matter previously infested it. Both the soul and the nonsoul are eternal existences. From a theological point of view, the basic dualism of the soul and the nonsoul in Jainism presupposes their deification.

The two elements possess at least some of the attributes traditionally assigned to deity. Thus, it may be said, Jainism's conception of the divine is dualistic.

Later Jainism, although it continues to be based philosophically upon the system of mind and matter just outlined, added elements of belief and practice which are not clearly contained in its earliest philosophy. Many of the gods of Hinduism have been reinstated, and Mahavira himself has been apotheosized. Jainism's founder, who was critical of the Hindu pantheon, now is considered an incarnation (*avatar*) in India like Rama and Krishna. Jainism currently features the worship of Mahavira and other deities in carefully prescribed ritual forms in their temples. The modern Jain quickly denies that he is an atheist; he believes that Jainism is more than a philosophy of existence—an authentic religion.

The question may be raised as to what constitutes a religion. Can a religion be essentially Godless? The answer to this question is difficult and ranges far beyond Jainism. Such a question is related, of course, to the discussion of the nature of religion in Chapter 1. Buddha, like Mahavira, did not believe in the traditional conceptions of God. Perhaps he did not believe in God at all. Similarly Confucius, who founded a religion which has claimed the loyalty of countless million of Chinese, was not a believer in God. Yet Buddhism and Confucianism are widely considered to be religions. In addition there is the problem of the pseudo-religions or secular religions, such as Marxism, psychoanalysis, nationalism, racism, Nazism, scientism. Some knowing people have been prone to classify a social phenomenon such as Marxism as an especially virulent form of religion. They claim that it has all the fundamental attributes of a religion except possibly the belief in a deity. Others, to continue with the same example, would claim that it actually has a deity: the legendary Lenin, or the dialectic process of history.

A religion, as we have seen in the first chapter, is a complex social phenomenon. The observer sees it as a social system. Three components make up the social system: doctrine, cultus, and communion. A religion consists of intellectually held beliefs regarding what is experienced as Ultimate Reality. It possesses a practical form consisting of ritual observances. It also expresses itself within a community of believers.

The distinction between a religion and nonreligion, however, may be inconsequential. A religion usually says that it is a religion, while a nonreligion clearly wishes to disassociate itself from being considered as a religion. Jainism, Buddhism, Confucianism declare themselves to be religions. They are accepted by many as such, including their adherents. But the nonreligions, such as Marxism, specifically disclaim being religions. In fact, the nonreligions are usually unsympathetic and even antagonistic toward social systems which claim to be religious. Jainism is a religion.

The Person

The foregoing discussion shows that the fundamental goal of the person is salvation (*moksha*). Salvation, however, is not easy to attain. The soul of man is laden with karmic matter. This in association with the soul prevents the individual from realizing his essential nature. The very real world of self, nature, and society has been set in motion by the conflict between spirit and matter. A small part of the matter attached to the soul is automatically cut off by the maturing of the matter. But the largest part remains unless it is consciously eliminated. The individual must depend solely upon himself for the purification of his spirit. No other agency can help him with his dilemma. But the person who succeeds in eliminating all karmic matter from his soul is assured of the highest happiness. This is a state in which he escapes from the cycle of birth and death and enjoys an absolute freedom of selfhood.

From this explanation of the human predicament, one then goes on to inquire how salvation can be achieved. The Jain answer is definite. There are three paths to salvation: right belief (*samyagdarsana*), right knowledge (*samyag-jnana*), and right conduct (*samyak-charitra*). These methods of emancipation are termed the three jewels (*ratnatraya*) in Jainism. Actually they are not three separate paths but in many respects a single way. In Hinduism there are similar paths which are held to be relatively separate; a person may find his salvation by following merely one of them. In Jainism, however, the three paths are considered a unity, and their simultaneous following is necessary for release. The three paths are compared to a ladder, with its two side supports and the rungs forming the steps. Right belief and right knowledge constitute the side supports. Right conduct forms the rungs. No right-minded person would seek to climb a ladder unless all three components were adequate.

To elaborate: Jainism declares that right belief cannot sharply be differentiated from right knowledge. On the contrary, it is basic to right knowledge. Unless the person possesses the proper belief he will not be able to secure that knowledge necessary to reveal the nature of things in detail. Right belief signifies the absence of wrong belief; therefore, wrong knowledge also is eliminated by possession of right belief. The latter obviously consists of Jain teachings, and the knowledge that results from such belief has been classified in Jainism into five categories: first, sense knowledge or knowledge of the self and nonself by means of the senses and the mind; second, scriptural knowledge or knowledge derived from the reading or hearing of the scriptures; third, clairvoyant knowledge or knowledge of distant times or places; fourth, mental knowledge or knowledge of the thoughts and feelings of others; and, fifth, perfect knowledge or omniscience. This last involves full or perfect knowledge without the limitations of time and space, and this sort of knowledge is appropriate to the soul in its pure and undefiled condition.

Right conduct is based upon the attainment of right knowledge, which in turn presupposes right belief. Each element is like a building block which, in proper position, helps to build one's salvation. Right conduct, like right belief and right knowledge, is powerful: it is able to destroy the entangling karmic matter around the soul. It consists of involved rules of discipline, at times like the Hindu Yoga, by which all evil movements of speech, body, and mind are weakened and destroyed. Right conduct has nonattachment and purity as its goal. Actually, according to Jain teaching, it takes two forms: the perfect or unqualified (*sakala*) and the imperfect or qualified (*vikala*). Unqualified right conduct is that practiced by ascetics whose rejection of the world is theoretically absolute. The layman practices qualified right conduct.

Jainism is both pessimistic and optimistic in its view of human nature. Insofar as it teaches that the person is subject to the restraints of matter, and is capable as a consequence of both giving and receiv-ing harm, it is basically pessimistic. Unlike some other religions it has rejected the sentimental or heroic divinizaton of man's nature. Man as he is found in society is no saint. He is not a simple expres-sion of the divine. On the contrary, man is "sinful." His sinfulness, however, derives not from the improper exercise of his will, as in the Adam and Eve myth. It is not merely the presence of ignorance, as the Greek philosophers thought, in part. Sinfulness, according to Jainism, represents the fundamental condition of human nature in which spirit and matter are in conflict. A similar view of the human situation has been expressed by St. Paul in the seventh and eighth chapters of Romans.

But in another sense, Jainism is boundlessly optimistic about man. Although it teaches a profound pessimism regarding his existential situation, it offers a sincere belief in the possible attainment of a sublime state of salvation. The limitations on the soul are not ac-ceptable to Jains; they seek through ascetic means to overcome them. They are strong in the rather innocent belief that the limitation of matter can be overcome. This belief is considered in some of the other living religions the ultimate heresy, the sin against the Holy Spirit, and a form of titanism which more consistently pessimistic religions have denied.

Jainism teaches that a pessimistic estimate of human nature can be transformed into an optimistic one on the basis of two forms of renunciation. First: world renunciation. Human society and all its manifestations are taken to be evil, or so laden with karmic matter as to limit constantly the pure existence of the soul. The personal ideal in Jainism is the monk, one who withdraws from the world and seeks, not its salvation, but his own. In this respect Jainism somewhat resembles early Epicureanism in Roman times and monas-ticism as it is practiced in several of the other living religions.

The second form is self-renunciation. The person is individually like the society. He is composed of soul and nonsoul. In order to attain salvation, he must seek to transcend his own physical being.

This he cannot do easily, but to that end must engage in the strictest control of beliefs, knowledge, and action. Thus, self-renunciation is practiced through self-discipline or ascetic controls.

Jainism's teachings on self-discipline are apparent in the five great vows for monks. All five call for self-renunciation. All are stated negatively as means of attaining the emancipation of the soul. The first vow (*ahimsa*) renounces violence or injury. The monk declares his willingness to refrain from killing any living being, whether movable or immovable. He will not consent to others' employing violence nor will he cause others to do harm. Second (*satya*), he pledges himself to renounce falsehood. He will not engage in lying speech as a result of either anger or greed, or of fear or hope of reward. Again, he will not consent to the speaking of lies by others nor will he cause others to speak lies. Third (*asteya*), the monk vows never to steal. He will take nothing that is not freely given, whether the object is little or much. He will not consent to others' thievery nor will he be a cause of it. Fourth (*brahmacharya*), he promises to be free from unchastity and all sexual pleasures. He will not give way to sensuality, nor consent to it in others, nor cause others to do either. Fifth (*aparigraha*), the monk denounces all worldly attachments whether to little or much, living or lifeless. He will not give himself to such attachments nor consent to it in others, nor cause others to do so.

Probably four of the great vows (excluding the one on chastity) were taught by Parshva, Mahavira's predecessor as a Tirthankara. Mahavira, according to Jain tradition, firmly believed that women are the greatest temptation in the world and, therefore, for the attainment of salvation (*moksha*) must be absolutely shunned. The fifth vow, however, which requires radical asceticism is probably sufficiently clear and inclusive so that the fourth would be covered even if it did not exist as a separate vow. By the terms of the five vows, and especially the fifth, Jainism establishes itself as strikingly different from some of the other living religions. It does not say that one should love the good and eschew the evil or that one should honor love and despise hate, and so forth. It teaches an absolute form of nonattachment. A person is required to give up any and all attachments, no matter whether previously he has acknowledged some as being more worthy than others.

In practice, however, Jainism made two kinds of compromises with the five great vows. First, it taught the four virtues upon which the observance of the five great vows are presumedly based: friendship with all living beings, delight at the sight of better qualified beings on the path of liberation, compassion for the afflicted, and tolerance or indifference to those who are uncivil or ill-behaved.

Second, Jainism provided of necessity a less severe code of conduct for its laymen. Although the vows for lay adherence are less strict, they are more numerous. The twelve principal vows for the laity are: never intentionally take the life of a living creature, never lie, never steal, never be unchaste, check greed by limiting one's wealth and giving away any excess, avoid temptation to sin by living as simply as possible, limit the number of things in daily use, be alert against avoidable evils, maintain periods of meditation, keep special times of self-denial, give certain days to monastic living, and be charitable, especially to the body of monks.

The doctrine of nonviolence (*ahimsa*), the initial vow for both monks and laymen, is a principal feature of Jainism. Although *ahimsa* is a part of several of the living religions, it reaches its fullest form and practice in Jainism. Some people even tend to equate Jainism and *ahimsa*. Others are inclined to believe that the greatest of the five great vows is not the last, but the first, for upon the observance of the first, all the others are achieved. *Ahimsa* has brought about some strange and noble behavior on the part of Jains. Their ritualistic avoidance of the killing of any living thing has led to seemingly bizarre practices, but it also possesses certain advantages. Jains, by reason of the principle, have not been able to become agriculturalists, to engage in butchering, fishing, brewing, or any other occupation in which life itself is directly or indirectly involved. As a consequence they have turned to careers in business, law, commerce, and property ownership and management. In these vocations in India and Pakistan they have been a notable success. Their wealth and social power are disproportionately large. Also their pecuniary activities are perhaps strengthened by some of the moral restrictions within the faith, such as the prohibitions on gambling, eating meat, drinking wine, adultery, hunting, and thieving. In general they form an affluent and upright community.

The Jains, also as a consequence of *ahimsa,* have been deeply attracted to social welfare and health services. They maintain institutions both for Jains and for non-Jains. Because of their wealth they are able to implement the phase of their religion that calls upon them to show compassion to all living things regardless of religion or caste.

Society

Jainism does not possess a highly developed set of teachings on society. Its doctrine of society may be simply stated: society should be renounced. The renunciation of the world depends upon a number of factors. The world, composed as it is of spirit and matter, is essentially evil. The person is similarly composed, but by renouncing the world and himself he is able to settle down to the primary task of saving himself. There is no thought within Jainism that the evil of the world can be successfully challenged. Karmic matter in that sphere is too extensive and frustrating. It is enough for the Jain to take his own evil seriously. Also, Jainism denounces society because it finds no purpose in it. The world of nature and society has not been created by a divine force and is not proceeding in any course to a successful consummation. It simply is, and little can or should be done about it. Although Jainism originally possessed a world outlook to some degree, it quickly lost it and any sense of the whole of humanity. This religion, furthermore, is nonprogrammatic so far as society is concerned. Aside from its social and health services it possesses no plan of social amelioration. It teaches no blueprint of an ideal society which will some day be achieved, through either human or divine effort or both. It is unconcerned with any devices or instrumentalities by which a better world may be won.

Despite the fact that the teachings of Jainism are centered in salvation for the individual, it early developed a sense and form of religious community. This is known as the *sangha* and is the oldest voluntary religious organization in the world. It preceded the development of the Buddhist *sangha*. Probably in its beginning it was formed by a group of the monastic elite within Jainism who for reasons of self-protection and edification withdrew together and constituted a corporate life for themselves. Gradually, however, the *sangha* was opened to all Jains as it is today. It represents a rough parallel to the church in Christianity.

The very existence of the *sangha* has had a number of consequences. A relatively deliberate body of knowledge or right beliefs had to be defined on which membership was based. This led to a continuing interest in the sacred scriptures of the religion. A place was required where the faithful could meet. Temples, therefore, were created for that purpose and to express in architecture, sculpture, and other art forms the essential ethos of the religion. Worship as an integrating experience for the faithful required delineation and establishment. Symbols of communication became important for the maintenance of the *sangha*. Another important factor was the priesthood. In Jainism one finds fully expressed the principle of *ecclesiola in ecclesia*: the inner group of devout believers within the larger group of the religious. In the full development of the *sangha*, this faith displays many features of religious organizations against which Mahavira originally protested in ancient Hinduism.

The meaning of the *sangha*, however, has been weakened in the historical development of Jainism through the strong propensity of the religion to split into sectarian groups. While Jains in the *sangha* may have a sense of unity and communion, they are unable to overcome their separateness from their own brethren. Thus the form by which cohesion was to be secured among them turned out to be an agency for keeping them apart.

Jainism as an independent religion was an offshoot from Hinduism. Its philosophy and practice provided Indians with a significant alternative to Hinduism.

ANNOTATED BIBLIOGRAPHY ON JAINISM

1 BRADEN, CHARLES. *Jesus Compared: A Study of Jesus and Other Great Founders of Religions.* Englewood Cliffs, N. J.: Prentice-Hall, 1957. A comparison of the founder of Christianity with the initiators of other living religions.

2 JAGMANDAR-LAL, JAINI. *Outlines of Jainism.* Cambridge, Eng.: The University Press, 1916. A simplified but useful account.

3 MEHTA, MOHANLAL. *Outlines of Jaina Philosophy.* Bangalore, India: Jain Mission Society, 1954. A study of Jain ontology, epistemology, and ethics.

4 SANGAVE, VILAS. *Jaina Community: A Social Survey.* Bombay: Popular Book Depot, 1959. A broad and dependable account of modern Jainism.

5 STEVENSON, MARGARET. *The Heart of Jainism.* New York: Oxford University Press, 1915. One of the best general sources on the subject.

Buddhism

A GLOSSARY OF BUDDHIST TERMS

Abhidhamma Pitaka	The third of the three *pitakas* or baskets, the Basket of Ultimate Things, of the Buddhist scriptures.
Anatta	The doctrine of the nonself or nonego, the ultimately unreal self.
Anicca	Impermanence or change.
Arahat	The saintly disciple, one who has fulfilled the conditions for salvation.
Bhikkhu	A monk.
Bhikkhuni	A nun.
Bodhi	Knowledge or enlightenment.
Bodhisattva	A future Buddha or a being destined for enlightenment.
Buddha	The enlightened one, title of the founder of Buddhism, given after his enlightenment.
Cetiya	A pagoda or *stupa*.
Ch'an	The Chinese corruption of *dhyana,* in turn corrupted in Japanese to become *Zen.*
Dalai	The title of the Grand Lama in Tibetan Lamaism, meaning "the sea" or that which is measureless.
Dharma	A duty or social obligation, an essential quality, or any reality.
Dhyana	Contemplation or meditation, same as *djhana.*
Djhana	Contemplation or meditation, the four higher states of consciousness.
Dukkha	Suffering, unhappiness, pain, sorrow.
Ge-Snen	Lay adherents in Tibetan Lamaism.
Ge-tsu	Deacons in Tibetan Lamaism.
Gen-ye	Newly-won adherents in Tibetan Lamaism.
Guru	A spiritual teacher who instructs disciples.
Hinayana	Another term for Theravada, a major division of Buddhism, meaning "the lesser vehicle."

117

Jihad	An Arabic term, meaning holy warfare.
Kalpa	A very long period of time, an aeon.
Karma	The principle of causality in moral experience.
Koan	An exercise in Zen Buddhism for breaking through the barriers imposed by rational thought.
Kshatriya	A member of the warrior or second highest caste in India.
Mahavagga	The Great Section of the Vinaya Pitaka.
Mahayana	A major division of Buddhism, meaning "the great vehicle."
Maitreya	The Buddha yet to come.
Mantra	The recitation of spells or verbal formulas.
Moksha	Ultimate release or salvation.
Mondo	A form of rapid question and answer used in Zen Buddhism, to escape the ordinary limits of thought.
Nat	The nature spirits of Burma.
Nikayas	Collections or writings of the Sutta Pitaka.
Nirvana	Enlightenment, freedom from self, the end of selfish desires, the state of salvation.
Pabbajja	Leaving the world to take up monastic life.
Paccekabuddha	One who has found salvation independently of others.
Panchas silas	Five negative precepts.
Parinirvana	Self-extinction.
Parrib-bajaker	A wandering mendicant.
Raja	King, chief, or ruler.
Sakyamuni	The wise one from the Sakya clan.
Samma ajiva	Right livelihood, fifth element of the Noble Eightfold Path.
Samma ditthi	Right understanding, first element of the Noble Eightfold Path.
Samma kammanta	Right action, fourth element of the Noble Eightfold Path.
Samma samadhi	Right meditation, eighth element of the Noble Eightfold Path.

Samma sankappa	Right attitude of mind, second element of the Noble Eightfold Path.
Samma sati	Right recollection, seventh element of the Noble Eightfold Path.
Samma vacha	Right speech, third element of the Noble Eightfold Path.
Samma vayama	Right effort, sixth element of the Noble Eightfold Path.
Sammasambuddha	One who devotes his enlightenment for the benefit of others.
Sumyaksambodhi	True or real enlightenment.
Sangha	The order of Buddhist monks.
Satori	The Zen term for enlightenment.
Shakti	The basic energy inherent in everything, a female deity.
Shastra	A document written by someone who is known by name.
Skandhas	The five factors constituting all physical and mental phenomena, including the individual person.
Stupa	Originally a burial mound; later, a more elaborate structure, also known as pagoda and catiya.
Sutra	A text spoken by the Buddha himself.
Sutta Pitaka	The second of the three pitakas or baskets, the Basket of Discourses, of the Buddhist scriptures.
Suvannabhumi	Burma, "the Golden Land."
Tanha	Desire, craving, or thirst.
Tantra	A manual which explicates the meaning of Tantrism, a form of Hinduism.
Tathagata	A title, meaning the truthfinder, given to the Buddha.
Theravada	A major division of Buddhism, meaning "the way of the elders."
Tripitaka	The Three Baskets or the scriptures of Buddhism.
Upasaka	A male lay adherent of Buddhism.
Upasika	A female lay adherent of Buddhism.
Vinaya	The code of monastic discipline.

Vinaya Pitaka   The first of the three *pitakas* or baskets, the Basket
of Discipline, of the Buddhist scriptures.

Yoga   The method and practice leading to union of the self
with the divine.

IV

BUDDHISM

INTRODUCTION

BUDDHISM IS THE third major religion to be born in India. Like Jainism, it was mothered by Hinduism. Although in the course of its development it spread to practically all parts of Asia, its origin and nature cannot be understood successfully without careful reference to Hinduism.

Buddhism is the only religion originating on the Indian subcontinent that became a world religion. Hinduism, Jainism, and Sikhism, which will be discussed in the next chapter, all originated but also to a large extent remained there. Buddhism, however, like Christianity and Islam, not only claimed to be an international religion; it is so in fact. Half a millenium before the life of Jesus, Buddhism became the first international religion.

Buddhism is clearly a creation of the genius of the Indian people. Yet following a time of triumph in the land it was rejected by the people, although various elements of its teachings were absorbed into Hinduism. But it found ready and permanent acceptance beyond the boundaries of its mother country. Its success outside India is based upon complex factors. One can see that in many places there was a spiritual need which Buddhism tended to fill. In China, for example, Confucianism was little concerned with individual salvation, but stressed social proprieties. Otherworldly Buddhism, however, pursued an intense interest in the eternal destiny of the individual. Nothing quite like it was known in China, and the Chinese as a consequence heard and accepted the story of personal salvation portrayed in Buddhism.

121

Buddhism is also the first international missionary religion. Its missionary mandate laid the basis for its universality. The Buddha himself was an active missionary, and he sought constantly to bring the good news of his teachings to others. Two responsibilities, moreover, were laid upon his disciples by the Buddha himself. First, each was required to leave the world (*pabbajja*) and to take up monastic orders, although not as a recluse. Second, he was commanded to go forth into the world to help people by bringing them the interpretation of life taught by the Buddha.

Both Buddhist monks and laymen engaged in missionary activity. Force as a method of extending Buddhism was not permitted and was unknown. Thus it is distinctive among the universal religions (Buddhism, Christianity, and Islam) in its denial of the use of force as a means to attain a greater end. In their history both Christianity and Islam have employed force to win converts. In Buddhism, by contrast, King Asoka, a Buddhist ruler of India in the third century B.C., renounced the use of force as a means of proselytizing Indians. He commissioned missionaries to go out singly, rather than in pairs as in early Christianity, to tell about the advantages of the religion.

The range of this religion is enormous. It comprises about twenty-five hundred years of complex development. During this time it spread to the north, east, and south of India and was absorbed into local customs and culture wherever it went. In addition, its appeal has been extended to countless thousands of people throughout the Western world as well as elsewhere.

Buddhism is a complex religion. It may be said to consist of a whole family of religions, so diverse are its manifest forms. It is primarily a school of spiritual achievement based upon prescribed techniques. It is also an expression of Asian moral philosophy which has shaped the actions of many millions in that part of the world. It includes mysticism, magic, ritual, forms of *yoga*, a detailed psychology, and other elements. Wherever it has gone in Asia it has contributed to the greatest art of each country. In China, for example, the art of the T'ang Dynasty, sometimes described as among the finest in the world, was largely Buddhist.

The kindliness of Buddhism toward all forms of life has set a standard for the ethical attitude of Asians. Its emphasis upon tol-

erance and gentleness merits some elucidation. Tolerance has always
been a primary characteristic of most schools of Buddhism. In this
respect it is somewhat like Hinduism, each having an open and
receptive mind toward new truths. Buddhists are especially tolerant
toward other religions. Their essential attitude is that any religious
system which is able to help men in their quest for salvation is indeed worthy of respect. While they have sought to persuade others
regarding the supreme advantages of Buddhism, they have done so
without assuming that they and they alone possess the only or final
truth. In fact, Buddhism has been so receptive to the truths of other
religions that it has included elements of them in its own system of
belief and practice. Thus Hindu deities are found in the religious
ceremonies of many Buddhists where the two religions have been in
direct contact with each other. Buddhism in China has absorbed
many Taoist beliefs and practices. Similarly in Japan, the gods and
goddesses found by Buddhism when it came to that country have
been incorporated into its Japanese form.

As we have seen above, Buddhism also exemplifies gentleness.
The warlike spirit is clearly discouraged in this religion. Tibetan culture, for example, has never regarded violence with favor. Among
other things it is there illegal to kill game for food, and blood-sports
are banned. Yet it must be admitted that Buddhism has on occasion
encouraged a spirit of militarism, although the consecrated monk is
held to stricter standards than the layman. In Japan, for example,
the layman often found that his Buddhism encouraged a type of
self-discipline amenable to the historic Japanese stress on combat,
as for example in the Samurai or military class of the feudal period.
The code of behavior governing the Samurai is known as Bushido,
and Zen Buddhism was one of the contributors to it. Warriors found
in Zen Buddhism an appealing stress upon austerity in personal
living and the virtue of thoroughness in achieving objectives that
nourished the code. Zen Buddhism also taught them how to use
meditative techniques to control their thoughts and feelings. In the
main, however, a spirit of gentleness has been introduced or strengthened wherever Buddhism exists. It clearly is on the side of the peace-
makers.

The enormous range of Buddhism is seen in the fact that it has acted historically as a cross-cultural binder in Asia. It is true that Europe—to take the example of another world region—has been divided culturally and nationally into many diverse groups and yet may be said to possess an ethos or set of common values which fundamentally unites it and makes of it a common cultural expression. Of other regions the same may be said to a greater or lesser degree. But aside from the generally common religion of Buddhism, there appears to be no very strong culturally binding force in Asia. The nations of India and China, for example, have developed independently. Only at certain minor points have their cultures blended. Buddhism appears to be the one great system of values which both nations readily understand and accept, and the same holds true for other Asian nations and cultural entities. Thus Buddhism is the most significant unifying agency in Asia today.

The religion has found favor, both now and in the past, among the ruling classes of Asian countries. In several, such as Thailand, Laos, and Cambodia, it is the state religion. A state's acceptance of an official religion is noteworthy testimony to its significance. Christianity and Islam as well as other faiths have also been accepted at various times and places as state religions, but Buddhism has always had a particular appeal to the ruling classes. Rulers, of course, were not able to enter monasteries or practice the purest monastic form of Buddhism. But in the long course of its historical development, the rulers of several countries have been converted to the religion and have actively given it their blessing and support.

Buddhism, like Jainism, came into being in the sixth century B.C. This century, as has been mentioned, was marked by as much creativity in the spheres of philosophy and religion as any other known to man. Buddhism as a great and appealing religion is not least among the achievements of that remarkable period.

While Buddhism and Jainism are independent religions, they bear comparison. Both go back, for example, to founders who did not try to found a religion. The Buddha, like Mahavira, reacted to the Hinduism of his day; he was a reformer who had no thought of establishing a new faith. Like Mahavira, he was not primarily interested in establishing an ecclesiastical organization, or even in spinning out an all-embracing philosophy of the universe. The Buddha was intensely personal in his religion. He himself sought salvation, but as a consequence of having sought his own salvation and found it, he extended his discoveries to others, bringing them within his fold. At that time a new religion was born.

Like Mahavira, it is by his title that Buddha is remembered; his personal name was Siddhartha Gautama. Mahavira means "great-souled," while Buddha means "the enlightened one." Neither was a member of the priestly caste which had contributed so heavily to Vedic and Brahmanic Hinduism; they were both members of the warrior (*kshatriya*) caste.

The two stood together in their rejection of the Hinduism of their time, although there is no evidence of their having met. They protested against the ancient Vedas, written in Sanskrit, a language which even by the sixth century B.C. was unintelligible to the common people. Instead Jainism and Buddhism produced their scriptures in the vernacular of various regions. Both leaders were repelled by the Hindu belief in many gods and the practice of elaborate sacrifices. The social distinctions of caste, which in the time of Mahavira and the Buddha were rapidly becoming fixed, were also rejected. In their place voluntary religious orders (*sangha*) were established. Philosophically, however, Buddhism and Jainism were no match for Hinduism. Both took refuge in an unconcern for the subtleties of the Hindu philosophic system, and are only inferentially philosophical systems to this day. Neither has any great taste for highly abstract thinking.

Yet both Buddhism and Jainism possess much in common with their mother, Hinduism. All three religions, despite strong examples to the contrary, are essentially world-rejecting or unworldly. They do not find political authority to be of such a nature as to satisfy the primary needs of men. The inevitable course of individual human action in this life is frustrating and negative. None of these three religions has ever been known for any organized program of social improvement.

The three also alike deny the intrinsic worth of the person. They agree that the human body is a drag upon the essential self, retarding it in its quest for freedom (*moksha*). They teach that the individual can be emancipated only through self-discipline. They are negative or even repressive so far as self-expression is concerned. By and large, they put the individual strictly on his own, whether he lives openly in society or in a monastery.

All three, moreover, are historically intertwined in belief and practice. A belief in *karma* and rebirth, for example, is held in common by all. They are all characterized by sectarianism and the lack of any central authority which formulates and enforces an orthodoxy.

Buddhism, however, speaks of the "middle path." The precise nature of this term will be explained later, but this faith takes a middle path *generally* in that it avoids the extremes presented by Hinduism and Jainism. One of these extremes, represented in Vedic Hinduism, permits the outright pursuit of worldly desires. At the other extreme, Jainism preaches a fundamentally severe form of self-discipline. Buddhism, as will be seen, represents the middle path. Buddhism also uses the "middle path" as a criterion of truth. Hinduism at one extreme, especially evident in the Upanishads, avers that the human mind is capable of demonstrating metaphysical doctrines. Jainism at the other extreme denies the possibility of piercing ignorance intellectually so as to attain the thresholds of transcendent reality. Buddhism views tolerantly all varying and conflicting metaphysical formulations. It does not oppose metaphysical efforts, yet expresses truths which are not confined to empirical conceptions of reality.

Buddhism is today one of the world's largest religions, but there is no precise way of knowing how many adherents it has. Students of the subject differ widely among themselves. Their estimates range from 100 to 440 million followers. Although it is a significant force in such countries as Burma, Cambodia, Ceylon, China, Japan, Korea, Laos, Nepal, and Thailand, it is difficult to know how many adherents are to be found in each country. China, for example, presents special difficulties on this score. Perhaps, all things considered, a figure of 150 million Buddhists is somewhere close to the truth.

Buddhism today is undergoing renewal. Thrown as this ancient faith is into the twentieth century in a region of the world whose major experience at present is social change, this religion is adapting itself with new vitality and fresh strength. Buddhism today is not what it has been at any time in its past. Certainly it is highly different from original Buddhism. One must look to the original to understand what developed into the present-day religion.

FOUNDER

At least two phases of Buddhism may be readily distinguished: first, the life and teachings of the Buddha; second, the religion and philosophy that grew up about the man and his teachings. The two cannot be equated. In fact, it is not possible within the bounds of scientific inquiry to portray the substance of either phase with precision. In both, fact and fancy are intertwined to such an extent that the final truth may never be known. The life of the founder, however, constitutes a proper starting point.

We have seen that "Buddha" is a title, "the enlightened one," conferred on the founder of the religion by those who recognized his spiritual attainment. The Buddha was born into the Gautama family and was given the name Siddhartha ("wish-fulfilling"). Apparently he was an Aryan of the *kshatriya* caste of the Sakya clan. This clan inhabited the area bordering on the Himalayas south of Nepal. His father, Suddhodana, was a native prince of some standing and wealth, possibly even a raja of the Sakya clan. His mother, Maha, a name filled with symbolism, gave birth to the Buddha in a fertile tract called the Lumbini Gardens near Nepal while on a journey.

It is difficult to date his birth and death. Many scholars maintain the dates 560 and 480 B.C., but chronology in general—including the birth and death dates of the Buddha—is a minor point of difference among the several sectarian groups within Buddhism. The available evidence is so disparate that nothing more than a tentative conclusion can be reached. There is agreement, however, that the Buddha was an actual historical personage.

Born in the town of Kapilavastu, about one hundred miles north of Benares, the Buddha led a life of ease and luxury. When he was sixteen years of age, according to tradition, his father built three palaces for him so that he could move from place to place with the sharply changing seasons. At nineteen he married Yasodhara. For ten years their union was not blessed with a son, but one was finally born, who was given the name Rahula. Yet the satisfactions of family life and the pleasant palace life did not still the spiritual restlessness of the young man.

Suddhodana, the Buddha's father, was highly protective of his son. Tradition has it that the father hoped that he would become a universal monarch, that is, emperor of all India. He encouraged his son to live within the palace walls, shielded from the evils of life by young servants. But this blissful state did not last. According to the legend the young prince, driving out of the palace with his charioteer, one day came upon a decrepit old man; this encounter stimulated his interest in old age and death. On another day while out for a drive he saw an unpleasantly diseased man; from this he learned the keen misery with which the lives of many are afflicted. On a third day the prince and his charioteer saw a dead man carried on a bier; this event pointed up the brevity of man's existence. These three sights made him spiritually sick. He realized that he, too, was a man bound to all the evils he had observed.

His father, however, did not give up. He persisted in trying to arouse the young prince from his depression. He provided him with tempting entertainment and all manner of pleasures; but the Buddha was unimpressed. A fourth observation, however, brought him an answer. As he sat under a tree by the roadside, the prince saw a yellow-robed monk walking toward him. From this ascetic, who according to legend may have been a manifestation of the divine, the Buddha received peace of soul. He learned from the monk how the evils of life can be overcome, and he felt that he had been given a mission not only to save himself but to release mankind from the world's suffering.

As a result of this experience, the Buddha resolved to renounce his privileged life and himself become a monk, seeking salvation. According to tradition, he bade farewell to his sleeping wife and son. He took his charioteer and his faithful horse and went from the

palace to the edge of the forest. There he cut off his long black hair
with his sword and sent his charioteer back to the palace with it.
He found a beggar with whom he exchanged his robes, and from
thenceforth went into the future, teaching salvation.

A six-year quest had begun.

There were two possible paths to salvation known to the Buddha
at this time. He tried them in succession. First he went to Rajagaha,
the royal city of the province of Magadha, and sought out two
priestly philosophers who were living ascetically in hillside caves.
One, Alara Kalama, taught him the eight stages of meditation by
which he might attain to the realm of nothingness. But the Buddha
did not find satisfaction in his teachings, for Alara Kalama was too
theoretical. What the Buddha sought was his own salvation.

The second ascetic, Uddaka Ramaputta, also expounded philosophical Brahmanism with the Buddha. He spoke of the state of
neither-perception-nor-nonperception, but the results were the same
as before. The Buddha was not able to secure his salvation (*moksha*)
through philosophical speculation.

The Buddha then settled in a grove at Uruvela, a monastic community near a river and a village. There he undertook for five years
the bodily asceticism which Jainism and other groups were then
teaching. By practicing physical austerities he sought to conquer
fear, subdue all lust of the flesh, control his mind, and find his salvation. He thought that the more he disciplined his body the clearer
his mind would become. He ate only "one hemp grain," a single
grain of rice, or one jujube fruit daily. He sat on a patch of thorns,
lay in a cemetery among decaying corpses, let filth accumulate ex-
cessively on his body, dressed in chafing garments, stood or squatted
in one posture for days, and in other ways sought to gain the blessed
state. So serious was he in his self-discipline that five other ascetics
were drawn to him in the hope that they might by copying him find
their own salvation.

The experience of self-denial, however, ended for the Buddha
one day when he fainted while going from his seat to the nearby
stream. His five friends thought he had died, but water from the
stream revived him. He remarked then that the way of mortifica-

tion had utterly failed. He decided that he would no longer take the Jain way, so with begging bowl in hand he became a wandering mendicant (*parrib-bajaker*). The five ascetics felt that he was giving up his quest for a life of relative self-indulgence. But the Buddha himself, after six years of search and after practicing the two best-known teachings of his time, was in his own opinion no nearer salvation than he had been when he left his palace. But these experiences had led him to consider a different means of emancipation.

Accepting a bowl of curds from a maid, Jujats, and having bathed and eaten, he entered a grove at Budhgaya and sat down at the foot of a tree. This later became known as the Tree of Knowledge or the Bodhi-tree. Here he began to meditate upon his past experience. He understood deeply that neither Hinduism nor Jainism had brought him release from desire. Neither was the path to freedom. What, then, was? Deep in a trancelike meditation he found the answer. Desire, said the Buddha, was the root cause of all human suffering, including his own. He desired both to live and to possess all manner of things. Even he, the Buddha, had thirsted (*tanha*) after his own salvation, but being defeated in his quest, he realized that at that very moment he was without desire. There was nothing he wanted. Suddenly the realization came upon him that he had indeed achieved salvation. He had been purged of all desire. This knowledge (leading to a state of ecstasy comprising four different phases) brought him to a condition of consummate purity and poised equanimity. In this exalted state his ignorance had been destroyed and knowledge had arisen; darkness was destroyed and light had broken forth. He was a twice-born man for whom the eternal burden of rebirth was no more. He had secured *nirvana*. He was no longer Siddhartha Gautama; he was the Buddha or the Enlightened One.

After resting under the Tree of Knowledge for seven days, he was confronted, according to tradition, by Mara, the Evil One. His temptation was: whether to keep his new-found ecstasy to himself or communicate it to the whole world. He had given up all to find salvation. He was a Buddha for his own sake (*paccekabuddha*), a state in which he concluded Mara wanted him to continue. Thus his saving experience would not be available to others. After painful and resolute analysis, however, he decided to be a Buddha for all (*sammasambuddha*). He defeated Mara by making the decision to return to the world in order to make his knowledge available to any and all.

Having made his decision to become the first missionary of Buddhism to the world, the Buddha thought first of his earliest teachers (*gurus*), Alara Kalama and Uddaka Ramaputta. These, however, had already passed away. He then decided to confront the five ascetics who had left him when he gave up his practice of physical austerity. He found them in the Deer Park in Benares. At first they supposed him to be in the same condition as when he had left, but they soon realized that he was a changed person. He engaged them in conversation for several days in an effort to explain his newfound salvation. His remarks are taken by Buddhists as constituting his first sermon, given on the night of the full moon of July on the topic, "Setting in Motion the Wheel of Righteousness."

In this famous sermon he spoke of the two extremes. One is a life given to pleasures. This the Buddha declared is degrading, sensual, vulgar, ignoble, and profitless. The second is a life given to mortifications. This extreme is painful, and also ignoble and profitless. The Buddha called the five to follow him. He spoke of himself as the Truthfinder (*Tathagata*). He told them that he had gained knowledge of the middle path, which leads to insight and wisdom. This middle path brings one to calm, knowledge, enlightenment, and even *nirvana*. He asserted that he was a monk who had achieved enlightenment (*arahat*) and called upon them to believe his claims and try his middle way.

The conversion of the five ascetics led to the founding of the Buddhist monastic order (*sangha*). A new stage of human possibility had been created for the Buddha, his five followers, and indeed for all mankind. Following several sermons in the Deer Park and the conversion of the five ascetics and a number of other persons, the Buddha ordained his first followers as missionaries. He instructed them to make converts of those who pledged to take their refuge in the Buddha, in his teachings (*dharma*), and in his order (*sangha*).

The Buddha, who opposed the popular teachings of Hinduism, readily made a place within the order for all persons. Here the caste system did not hold. Members of all castes were received into the order upon taking the pledge. Thus the new movement had a socially democratizing effect upon north India. Women, however, were taken into a separate order of nuns (*bhikkhunis*); apparently the Buddha was somewhat reluctant to admit them into the faith. He is reported to have said that their admission would materially shorten the life of the Buddhist religion, yet it is a fact that he accorded them equal opportunity with men for the attainment of salvation.

The Buddhist ministry continued mainly in northeast India for forty-five years and during this time won a large number of converts. As the Buddha reached the age of eighty, his followers hung more carefully upon his utterances. His disciples sought instructions from him on a number of topics. Ananda, for example, asked him for directions as to the future of the order, but the Buddha refused to concern himself with this. He warned Ananda against anyone who was too preoccupied with leading the sacred community, and redirected his disciple's thought to the individual quest for salvation. By one word or another, he left the impression with his followers that he knew his end was coming.

Some time later, on his way to Kusinara, the Buddha entered the household of Hunda, a goldsmith. The latter prepared a special meal for him and his followers, of which the principal ingredient may have been pork. (Some claim that his death was a result of indigestion through eating pork.) Following the meal, however, the Buddha went on toward Kusinara. But he was too ill to continue. He lay down between two sal trees, comforted Ananda particularly, and spoke with the other disciples. His last words were to the effect that decay is inherent in all things and that the brethren should work out their own salvation with diligence. Following this declaration, according to tradition, he entered the four higher states of consciousness (*djhana*), and when he had come into the fourth stage he passed away.

In the foregoing account of the life of Buddha the blend of fact and fiction is openly and generally recognized. On a number of points there are varying legends. While some critical scholarly work has been carried out on the life of Buddha, much remains to be done. At present, therefore, scarcely any account can claim to be definitive.

The apotheosis of the Buddha following his death is one of the amazing features of Buddhism. The Buddha who did not recognize a personal deity, who eschewed any form of worship, and who never prayed, became himself a god who is worshiped in part through prayer by tens of millions of Buddhists. He who began by not seeking to found any religion became the central symbol of a religion. His deification may derive in part from the highly sacrificial way in which he gave himself to the saving of the world. The adoration of the Buddha may also be a result of other factors, such as the particular formulation of his doctrine regarding the possibility of overcoming the evil of this life. Surely the founding of Buddhist congregations (sangha) did much to bind his followers together. But the historical fact is that the human Buddha became the divine Buddha.

Those who believe in the Buddha's godlike quality insist that he did not come into the world for the first time in 560 B.C. Like all human beings, it is claimed, he had undergone countless births and had known the nature of the world as an animal, a man, and as a god. His achievement of *nirvana* actually took more than three long aeons (*kalpas*), during which he prepared for his final achievement by practicing virtues in all possible ways. Thus his preexistence is marked, according to tradition, by a developing divinity.

The concept of the divinity of the Buddha also gained suport from the uncommon events of his lifetime. His disciples believed that he suffered from no fault and was perfectly thoughtful and enlightened. They described his mildness and kindness as unequaled in all the world. They proclaimed him a king of universal kings, a conqueror. He was able, according to tradition, to appear and disappear at will. He performed various miracles: gave sight to the blind from birth, while the deaf from birth received their hearing; the crippled from birth had the use of their limbs restored; and the fetters of prisoners broke and fell off.

Down through history, Buddhists have disagreed on the degree of veneration to be accorded to the Buddha. One group is inclined to accept and teach the human Buddha, who called in his dying words for his disciples to be self-reliant rather than dependent upon any divine being. Another group, however, has developed theological doctrines which assert that the Buddha is indeed the divine savior of the whole world. By this sect of Buddhism he has been extensively idolized. In fact, there are more images of the Buddha in the world than of any other divinity.

HISTORY

The history of Buddhism is very complex; the following sketch will provide only the barest outline. A number of factors have created this complexity. First, Buddhism was not able to maintain a common following, but split into various groups, each of which interpreted the faith in its own way. Second, it spread to many countries of Asia and became identified with their cultures. Some attention, therefore, must be given to the distinctively national forms of Buddhism as well as to the denominational or "school" developments within the religion.

Following the death of the Buddha, the First Great Council was convened at Rajagaha. Its primary task was to define the teachings of the movement's founder. The aged Kassapa presided, and Upali —a prominent disciple—repeated the rules of discipline of the order. These rules are called the Vinaya Pitaka. Ananda recited the so-called Basket of Sermons, the Sutta Pitaka. Also recited was the *pitaka* of metaphysics, psychology, and philosophy which in Buddhist history is known as the Abhidhamma Pitaka. The five hundred leading *arahats* or monks attending the council, which was held in the Sattapanni cave, joined their leaders in reciting and compiling the teachings of Buddha into a systematic format. The result became the canon of Buddhism. In Sanskrit the Buddhist bible is known as the Tripitaka. Its contents consist of the threefold divisions of rules, sermons, and teachings previously mentioned. Of course, the council did not commit the canon to writing, but by recitation memorized it and passed it on over the succeeding centuries to others.

The First Great Council is thought by some scholars to be legendary rather than historical. But assuming its factuality, it probably did not take place after the fashion of modern church councils in Christendom. Rather, it may be said to have been a gathering of interested monks who went informally about their tasks in a cooperative way.

About a hundred years later the Second Great Council was convened at Vesali under the patronage of King Kalasoka. The basis for this council was the fact that a group of the faithful found the existing rules too irksome and demanded that they be relaxed. These monks advocated comfortable beds, an evening meal, private confession in place of the bimonthly confession before the chapter of monks, and permission to possess silver and gold. In addition, an important doctrinal difference was expressed. The orthodox leaders of the *sangha* saw honor attained only as a consequence of strict observance of the rules. The schismatic minority, however, asserted that Buddhahood was already within the believer; it was not something to be achieved from without—it simply needed to be developed. The debate at the council rested upon varying interpretations of the Tripitaka, each side believing itself faithful to the canon.

The unorthodox minority was finally defeated and held its own council to give form and authority to its heretical teachings. The followers of this progressive sect were known as the Mahasanghikas. They provided a basis in belief and practice for the Mahayana school of Buddhism which developed in most of Asia and exists widely today. The orthodox group, called the Sthaviravadas, were forerunners of the other main body of both historical and current Buddhism, found mainly in southern Asia, called the Theravada (or Hinayana) school.

The divisions of early Buddhism might have wreaked utter havoc in the new movement had it not been for Asoka Maurya, grandson of Chandragupta, who as an army officer founded an Indian empire by defeating the Greek forces of Alexander after the latter's death in Babylon. Asoka continued his conquests until practically the

whole of ancient India was his domain. As a result of his bloody
conquests, however, he underwent a striking change of mind. The
cruelties of warfare revolted him, and hearing of the gentle teachings of the Buddha, he became a lay adherent (*upasaka*) of the religion. Thus both religion and goverment had a single head. Through
his conversion, Buddhism grew from a popular teaching of northeast India to be the religion of all India.

Asoka took his religion seriously. He was a man of peace who
called upon his own people and those of surrounding countries to
accept Buddhism as the greatest of gifts. He publicly taught the
dharma or teachings of the essential Buddhist way of life. He established himself as an example of a layman of Buddhist virtues
by building hospitals, digging wells and reservoirs, establishing a
series of *stupas* or memorial mounds commemorating the life of the
Buddha and of former Buddhas, and stimulating the followers to
produce the various forms of art that distinguished his reign. Later,
it is said, he was ordained as a monk (*bhikkhu*), but could
not assume the obligations of that state since his administrative
duties required him to continue as a layman.

Asoka was not a theologian or philosopher. He did not expound
Buddhism with new or profound interpretations. These matters he
left to the more learned and contemplative monks. His strength
lay in other directions. During his forty-year reign he succeeded in
persuading many Indians to adopt his religion and practice it with
vigor and sincerity. He exhorted his people with a series of edicts,
some of which were cut in stone in widely scattered places. These,
thirty-five in all, offered practical guidance for everyday living. They
provided a code of Buddhist conduct for the masses of India.

Under his sponsorship the Third Great Council was held at
Pataliputra (Patna), under the leadership of Tissa. This council
had two aims, First, it sought to overcome the growing number of
heresies that continued to plague Buddhism even under the benign
reign of Asoka. The principal basis for the divisions continued to
hinge on the looser as against the stricter interpretation of the
Buddha's teachings. There were those who felt the religion was in-
humanly rigid, and these wanted to liberalize it. On the other hand,

the continuing and larger group of the orthodox were concerned lest the original deposit of teachings be dissipated in careless belief and practice.

A second concern was with canonical matters. A thousand *arahats* (monks) assembled at this council and recited the entire canon over a period of nine months. By this means of common acknowledgement of the scriptures, the teaching of Buddhism was further defined. Plans also were laid at this time for sending missionaries throughout India and even to other lands.

Asoka was a strong believer in the Buddhist missionary movement. Supported by the advocacy of missionary activities of the Third Council, he sent official missionaries to many places in India where Buddhism was not known. In addition his missionaries went to Cyrene, Egypt, Greece, Syria, and Ceylon. One is tempted to think of him as a parallel to Paul in early Christianity, for it was Asoka's organizing ability and his sense of the universal mission of Buddhism that changed it from a localized sect into a major religion embracing many different peoples. In fact, if Asoka had not organized its missionary movement, it might today be merely an historical curiosity, for in time Buddhism was virtually to disappear from India. By that time, however, it was strongly entrenched elsewhere.

After the death of Asoka, Buddhism entered a period of general decline in India, and despite several efforts at renewal remained in decline until the seventh century A.D., when as the result of several circumstances it almost wholly vanished from the great subcontinent. One high point occurred in the second or first century B.C. under King Milinda (the Greek Menander), who wrote a masterful defense of the main teachings of the orthodox school. The Syrians, Greeks and Scythians in this time came into the Punjab in great numbers where they became dominant, creating a Greco-Bactrian culture of some significance. Their King Menander became in the local tongue King Milinda. The purpose of his document (*Milinda Panha*) was to shore up the wavering beliefs of some of the Buddhists of his time. He wrote his document in question-answer form.

Following the reign of Milinda, however, the Kushans conquered northwest India and for a time threatened the development of the faith. But the conversion to Buddhism of Kanishka, one of the greatest of the Kushan kings, greatly revived the religion in that region. He convened a council for the purpose of harmonizing the growing differences between the two main schools of Buddhist thought. It did not succeed, however, and King Kanishka's council is not recognized as a major council by Theravadan Buddhists, and is therefore not reckoned in the list of the great councils.

Other teachers and leaders arose during the succeeding centuries who in one way or another reinterpreted Buddhism and forwarded the religion despite its generally waning power. Its decline in India came, nevertheless, inevitably. A major reason for it was the vitality of the Hindu tradition. Even during the golden days of Buddhism, Hinduism was not extinct. Tolerant, flexible, and open-minded, it had great ability to persist. Its remarkable power of absorption was much in evidence during the centuries of competition with its rival. It succeed finally in overcoming Buddhism, reestablishing the caste system, converting Buddhist temples in Hindu shrines, and using Buddhist teachings to make Hinduism more attractive to the masses.

Buddhism was also in decline for internal reasons. The strict injunctions to self-discipline were difficult for large numbers of people to obey. Compromise between the demands of the world and the idealistic principles of the Buddha became a regular practice. Even the monks relaxed. As the order (sangha) grew in size and strength, the monks laid less stress upon renunication and sacrifice and more upon academic pursuits and religious celebrations. The very success of the faith led it into compromise with popular beliefs and practices. As a consequence its supporters suffered a growing number of divisions. Sectarianism was rife. Buddhism had lost its savor.

Buddhism declined in India also because of the Muslim invasion. The followers of Islam conquered great sections of the country, ruining monasteries, shrines, and schools as they went and killing the distinctively clad Buddhist monks with a religious zeal (jihad). Islam, a missionary faith which uses force if necessary to gain converts, severely persecuted the adherents of the indigenous religions it found in India: Hinduism, Jainism, Buddhism. The last was all but crushed. Fortunately, however, through the missionary efforts of Asoka and others, it survived and flourished elsewhere.

The historical expansion of Buddhism cannot be understood without an appreciation of its two major schools: Theravada and Mahayana. The Theravada is found mainly in Ceylon, Burma, Thailand, Cambodia, and Laos; the Mahayana largely in China, Tibet, and Japan. The chief doctrinal differences between the two schools have been hinted at and will be discussed presently. At this point it is sufficient to note that they differ in several ways. Mahayana Buddhism has developed intricate philosophical systems, while Theravada is less concerned with abstract thought. Again, Mahayana bases its teachings upon Sanskrit sources; these are one of the marks of intellectualism within Buddhism. Theravada Buddhism depends upon Pali scriptures, a vernacular available to a larger number of people. The former also stresses the importance of the various Bodhisattvas or gods, while the latter is more strict in its dependence upon the human figure at the core of Buddhism, the Buddha himself.

Ceylon. Mahinda, Asoka's son (some say his brother) brought Buddhism to Ceylon. King Tissa (not the Tissa previously mentioned) was on a hunting expedition when he met Mahinda at Mihintale, a few miles from Anuradhapura, the capital city of the time, and arranged a treaty of friendship between himself and Asoka. In the course of the new-found relationship, Mahinda preached the true doctrine (*dharma*) to Ceylon's king and his followers. Great numbers of Ceylonese were converted. A monastery was built in the royal park for the Theravadan order, and from it Buddhism spread throughout Ceylon. In time the island became one of the great centers of Buddhism.

Some time later Sanghamitta, Mahinda's sister, came to the Sinhalese court bringing with her a cutting from the famed Tree of Knowledge (*bodhi*). At the request of King Tissa's daughter, who expressed a desire to become a nun, she also founded the order of Buddhist nuns (*bhikkhuni*) in Ceylon.

Near the monastery King Tissa built the Thuparama Pagoda

(*stupa*) to enshrine a collarbone of the Buddha. This relic was a gift from Asoka and has through the centuries been considered one of the great physical centers of Buddhism. In the third century A.D. a tooth of the Buddha was brought to Ceylon and placed in the Temple of the Tooth at Kandy.

The Fourth Great Council was held in the rock cave of Matale, sponsored by the Sinhalese *sangha* about 25 B.C. About five hundred monks convened to further refine the religion's canon and preserve it in writing. In the following centuries considerable effort was made to interpret the written canon. In the fourth century A.D., for example, Buddhaghosa, a Brahman convert to Buddhism from Gaya, became the first great Buddhist commentator. He translated the commentaries of the times from Sinhalese into Pali, the original language of the canon, and was joined by other scholars who consolidated and systematized the available commentaries.

Until the Portuguese arrived in Ceylon in 1505 A.D., Buddhism flourished there. Its attainments in piety and learning were acknowledged through out southeast Asia. But the religion lost much of its power during the period of occupation by the Portuguese, and later the Dutch and the British. At one point it became so weak that monks from Thailand had to be imported to renew its strength and influence in Ceylon.

Burma. The development of Buddhism in Burma (*suvannabhumi* or "the Golden Land") is difficult to trace. One tradition has it that Asoka sent his missionaries there. Another says that Buddhaghosa was the source of Burmese Buddhism, although Ceylonese records do not reveal the fact. For about sixteen centuries after the Buddha, Buddhism in Burma was apparently a mixture of the Theravada and Mahayana schools. This in turn was combined with an indigenous kind of nature worship (*nat*), which involved propitiation of malevolent forces in nature. Buddhism's message of personal superiority in an evil world was probably an attractive innovation in Burma.

Another version of the inception of Buddhism in Burma is contained in the Vinaya Pitaka. According to this account from the sacred scriptures, Tapassu and Phallika happened to be near the place where the Buddha received his enlightenment. They offered him his first food and became his disciples; he, in turn, gave them a few hairs from his head which they brought back to Rangoon and placed in a pagoda (*cetiya*), later called the Shwedagon Pagoda. This impressive shrine in the heart of Rangoon is today one of the foremost objects of Buddhist pilgrimage.

A great turning point in the history of Buddhism in Burma occurred in the time of King Anawrahta of Pagan (1044-1077 A.D.), who was converted by Shin Arahan, a wandering monk and strong advocate of Theravada Buddhism. The converted king, somewhat like Asoka in India before him, sought to make his kingdom a Buddhist showplace. His influence lasted for about two centuries, when the country fell to the armies of Kublai Khan. Buddhism, however, became prominent again in the sixteenth century A.D., when the British took control. In 1871, during the reign of King Mindon, the Fifth Great Council was held in Mandalay, and one result of it was the inscription of the Pali text of the canon on 729 marble slabs placed at the foot of Mandalay Hill. The council reflected the influence in its cosmopolitanism that the several invaders of Burma had brought with them.

Burma was also the meeting place of the Sixth Great Council, held in Rangoon, beginning on the full-moon day of May, 1954, and ending two years later on the twenty-five-hundredth anniversary of the founding of Buddhism. As in past councils, the Tripitaka was recited in Pali. Steps were taken to have the sacred scriptures of Buddhism translated into other languages.

Thailand. Traditionally Buddhism is thought to have arrived in Thailand through the efforts of two Asokan missionaries, Sona and Uttara. Probably its penetration was relatively easy, since even from pre-Buddhist times the Thais had been trading regularly with Indians. While the initial Buddhism in Thailand was Theravada, the introduction of Mahayana Buddhism took place through contacts with Java and Cambodia. Because of the interest of a succession of Thai kings, however, Theravada Buddhism became dominant and is influential in Thailand even today.

Cambodia. This country partly follows Theravada Buddhism, as was perhaps to be expected, since what is now geographically Cambodia was until about the thirteenth century A.D. an extension of India. During the early dominance of Hinduism in India, that religion was found also in Cambodia as well as Laos, Vietnam, and elsewhere. When Theravada Buddhism came to the fore in India, it too became known in Cambodia. The Buddhism of Thailand, Ceylon, and Burma also helped to shape the religious life there.

In addition, Buddhism spread in one way or another to Laos, Vietnam, Malaysia, Sumatra, Java, Bali, Borneo, and elsewhere in southeast Asia. In these areas both major schools of Buddhism exist. In Vietnam, for example, because of its geographic proximity to China, the Mahayana form is found.

China. According to tradition, Buddhism reached China in the first century B.C., probably brought by traders who followed the routes northward from India and eastward to the Gobi Desert. Chinese Buddhists say that the Emperor Ming Ti in 61 A.D. sent eighteen messengers (some say twelve) to India, as a result of a dream, to investigate Buddhism. After spending eleven years in that country the group returned with images of the Buddha, some of the religion's writings, and two Buddhist monks.

The scriptures, translated by an Indian scholar into Chinese, were from the Mahayana school, and the translation was readily received by the Chinese. Even Confucian and Taoist scholars of the day were in tensely interested in the written accounts of Buddhism.

The monks founded a monastery and were later joined by others. The principal activity of the Indian monks and their Chinese disciples in those days was that of translating Sanskrit Buddhist books into Chinese. It is said that more than 350 books were translated within three centuries.

Yet the development of Buddhism in China was relatively slow. After all, China possessed one of the most complex and advanced cultures in the world. Confucianism and Taoism were already widely accepted by the educated Chinese. It was natural for them to look askance at an essentially foreign intrusion. The Chinese religions and Chinese culture itself had had no experience with monastic life; neither Confucianism nor Taoism taught world renunciation.

The life of a monk or nun meant that the Chinese would be called upon to forgo their primary task of parenthood, a responsibility upon which was built the highly developed Chinese sense of filial respect. These and other elements within the culture presented formidable challenges to the invading religion.

Yet Buddhism possessed certain advantages for the Chinese. The Mahayana form was much more highly developed philosophically than was Confucianism. It presented a stimulus to the intelligentsia, and appealed strongly to those who felt the need to seek their personal salvation. As we have seen, Buddhism is not a religion of social propriety but of individual salvation; China needed such a religion, and in time the Chinese people opened its arms to the new faith.

Buddhism failed to make headway in China during the approximately four centuries of the two Han dynasties (roughly 200 B.C. to 200 A.D.), because during that period China was effectively united. The major energies of the era went into building a practical Confucian society. The Three Kingdoms (200-280 A.D.) came in the wake of the dissolution of the second Han dynasty. During the three centuries that followed, migrating tribes of central Asia overran China, creating political and social disunity. Leading Chinese, especially the scholarly and the religious, were disillusioned. They saw little prospect of realizing the essentially optimistic hopes of Confucianism. Disheartened, they became eager subjects for the mysticism of Taoism and, indeed, for the Buddhist faith. Worldly frustration led to the acceptance of other-worldly Buddhism.

Buddhist missionaries, moreover, brought a religion which appealed no less to the great masses in China. The doctrine of the after life, relatively weak in Confucianism and appealing to a people in confusion, was given clear and attractive meaning in Buddhism.

Several leaders were influential in strengthening the religion in China. Kumarajiva, an outstanding translator of the fourth and fifth centuries A.D., secured broad support among the Chinese through his attractive translations. Many Chinese became monks as a consequence of his work, and a Chinese branch of the *sangha* was formed. Dependence upon India and other Buddhist lands was greatly reduced, and Chinese Buddhism became a force, especially throughout northwest china.

In the sixth century A.D. the Buddhist mystic and saint, Bodhidharma, an Indian Buddhist from Conjeeveram, near Madras, brought the Chinese a stirring personal and scholarly exemplification of Buddhism. He was not entirely in sympathy with the prevailing Buddhism, but sought to purify it by returning to the spirit of the original teachings of the Buddha. He advocated no dependence upon mere words and letters, a special transmission outside the scriptures, a direct pointing to the soul of man, and the possibility of seeing into one's own nature. These teachings, which he called *dhyana,* he claimed were consonant with the Buddha's own. His school was named from the Chinese corruption of *dhyana ch'an,* which in the course of time was corrupted by the Japanese into *zen.* For in the twelfth century this form of Buddhism passed into Japan, although it still remains a vital religious force in China.

The history of Chinese Buddhism is in large part a history of Buddhist sects. Of these there have been many, each with its own particular emphasis. Some scholars claim that they grew up as a consequence of efforts to arrange the canon of Buddhist sacred scriptures. Thus, each arranger of the canon sought to give prominence to a sacred scripture or an arrangement of them which to him most ideally expressed the Buddhist religion. But other scholars are quick to point out the relation of sectarianism to the changing cultural features of Chinese society. An adequate account of the Chinese sects is beyond the scope of this book, although three Buddhist schools of thought will be presented later in this chapter for illustrative purpose. These, however, are not basically Chinese in origin or expression.

Korea. Buddhism came to Korea from China in the fourth century A.D., and its form was essentially that of the Chinese. Although it flourished for several hundred years, it was set back in the thirteenth century by a wave of Confucianism from China. In the fifteenth century the ruler of Korea banished institutional Buddhism from much of the country. What remains today in Korea is almost wholly Zen Buddhism.

Japan. Buddhism was introduced into Japan in the sixth century A.D. by the ruler of Korea, who sent a delegation to bring an image of the Buddha to the emperor of Japan. Initially the religion was resisted, and it was not until the regency of Shotoku Taishi (593-622 A.D.) that it made significant headway. Shotoku Taishi as a strong advocate of Buddhism was to some degree the Japanese counterpart of Asoka in India. He became its patron, and in the city of Horyuji, which he built, he established a monastic settlement whose architecture has been widely imitated down to the present day.

Although the Buddhism of Japan came initially from Korea, its relations with Chinese Buddhism have always been direct and vital. The Japanese sent monks to China in order to study Buddhism at first hand. Deputations of monks from China also came to teach in Japan. As a consequence Japanese Buddhism represents practically all the Chinese Buddhist schools of thought, most of which fall within the category of Mahayana Buddhism.

For eleven centuries—more than a thousand years—Buddhism was the dominant religion of Japan. In the seventeenth century, however, the Tokogawa Shoguns revived Shintoism, Japan's native religion. The renewed Shintoism had its own attractions and in addition launched a vigorous opposition to the several existing forms of Buddhism. The popularity of Buddhism waned. In the nineteenth century, the influx of Christian missionaries into Japan also to some extent dampened the popularity of Buddhism. Following the tremendous readjustments necessitated by the Second World War, Buddhism began to take stock, to check its decline, and to strengthen its acceptance among the Japanese people.

The history of Buddhism in Japan, as elsewhere, cannot be fully understood without a recognition of the various sects into which Buddhists' interests and energies have been channeled. These, however, are many and varied, and thus beyond the scope of this book. One, Zen Buddhism, will be briefly commented upon presently.

Tibet. Buddhism was not introduced into Tibet until the seventh century A.D. Prior to that time cultural isolation, induced in large part by the Himalayan range of mountains, kept Tibet and India apart. According to tradition, a certain king of Tibet, Songtsan-

Gampo, had two queens, one from Nepal and the other from China. Both were devout Buddhists who acquainted him with their faith and encouraged him to accept it. The king sent representatives to India to study the religion and invited Buddhist monks from various countries to intoduce Buddhism into Tibet. In addition, he established many temples and monasteries.

But a century went by before the new faith caught on in Tibet. In the eighth century A.D. King Trisong-Detsan invited for a visit a certain Santarakshita, a noted Buddhist saint and philosopher of the time as well as principal of the Buddhist school at Nalanda. Upon the arrival of the Indian teacher, Tibet suffered a variety of calamities: famine, epidemics, floods, and storms. The king sent the teacher away to Nepal. But before leaving, Santarakshita suggested to him that he invite Padmasambhava, a great Indian mystic, who he believed would be able to overcome these misfortunes. Padmasambhava came to Tibet, and providentially the disasters ceased. He was looked upon as a great hero. Later Buddhism in the distinctive form of Lamaism became an even stronger force in Tibet.

The development of Buddhism has not been restricted to Asia. The influence of the religion in Europe and North America, though not strong, is yet evident. For example, estimates of the number of adherents to Buddhism in America vary from 80,000 to 165,000. But Buddhism as a system of belief and practice has attracted the attention of many more Americans who have not become converts, but maintain an interest in it as they would in all important systems of thought and behavior. Not many Westerners have adopted the saffron robe of the Buddhist monk, but an increasing number have been attracted to this faith as their knowledge and appreciation of world culture has grown.

Because of political events in recent years the fate of Buddhism in China and Tibet is presently ambiguous. But elsewhere in Asia the religion is undergoing renewal.

Efforts have been made to bridge the gap between Theravada and Mahayana Buddhism. Buddhist scholars have recently been inclined to think of these as complementary aspects of a common faith. They also have been meeting together on occasion to examine their heritage. International bodies have sprung up in each division so that a broader perspective can be achieved. In Japan there is the Young Buddhist Association, comparable to the West's Y.M. and Y.W.C.A's and to social welfare agencies. Buddhism has returned to India and Pakistan through the activities of a world-wide missionary movement. There is a World Fellowship of Buddhists for World Buddhism which has met biennially since 1950. So, in these and other ways, Buddhism is today a significantly living religion.

SCRIPTURES

The sacred scriptures of this religion are based upon the teachings of the Buddha. They are called the Tripitaka or the Three Baskets. Each of the Three Baskets comprises a separate section of the whole. The first is known as the Basket of Discipline (Vinaya Pitaka). The second is the Basket of Discourses (Sutta Pitaka). And the third is the Basket of Ultimate Things (Abhidhamma Pitaka). The Tripitaka would comprise in English translation more than a dozen large books. It is not available in its entirety in English; in fact not all of it has been published in the original Pali.

The first Pitaka, the Basket of Discipline, briefly outlines the rules and regulations by which the conduct of monks (*bhikkus*) and nuns (*bhikkhunis*) is governed. Within it may also be found detailed descriptions of the life and ministry of the Buddha and of the development of the early form of the *sangha*. This Pitaka is divided into five books. The first contains an explanation of each rule and the manner in which it came to be enunciated, along with a listing of special cases and exceptions. The second book, similar to the first, deals with minor offenses. The third book covers the life of the monk or nun in the order: the rules for admission to the order, the ritual or ordination, details of dress, and the conduct of special monastic activities. The fourth book is concerned with the duties of teachers and novices and provides information regarding their supervision. The fifth book is primarily a commentary on the third book which sometimes is called the Great Section (Mahavagga). It consists of accounts of the events that took place after the enlightenment of the Buddha.

The second Pitaka, the Basket of Discourses, consists of addresses given by the Buddha. It is composed of five collections (Nikayas). These cover a wide variety of topics, such as the training of the disciple, the Buddha's austerities, his enlightenment, his early teachings, description of the Noble Eightfold Path, discourses on the six senses, descriptions of the "prize aggregates" (combinations of existence), comments on heresies, birth stories, the lives of saints, and modes of conduct. The content and language of the Second Basket are most popular with Buddhist laymen, since they are most available to them by reason of language and are of interest because they discuss perennially practical matters.

The Dhammapada in the fifth collection of the second Pitaka is well known and widely read wherever Buddhism is followed, and has in addition been read and admired throughout much of the world. Best known of all Buddhist scriptures, it teaches self-reliance. The faithful follower is enjoined to make his own way spiritually, conquering passion, hatred, and folly.

The third Pitaka, the Basket of Ultimate Things, is concerned with the more philosophic teachings of the Buddha. The topics discussed in this Pitaka are expressed in the titles of the seven books which compose it: Enumeration of Phenomena, Book of Analysis, Treatise on the Elements, Book of Human Types, Points of Controversy, Book of Pairs, and Relations.

The third Basket is the scholar's document. It describes the philosophic basis of existence, with its interest centered in the primary value of *nirvana*. Abstract thought is engaged in only as a means of illuminating the ultimate human goal of *nirvana*. Thus the third Basket is not as popular as the first two, since its reasoning is more sophisticated and requires a substantial background of education and experience for understanding.

Buddhists analyze the Tripitaka through the use of a variety of special terms. They speak of *dharma* (*dhamma* in Pali) as referring to the doctrinal elements within the sacred scriptures, while *abhidhamma* is employed to refer to advanced doctrines. *Vinaya* is a term applied to monastic discipline. A *sutra* (*sutta* in Pali) is a text which claims to have been spoken by the Buddha himself and always begins with the words: "Thus have I heard at one time." The "I" here refers to the Buddha's disciple Ananda, who it is assumed was responsible for all the records of the Buddha following his death. Historical scholarship shows, however, that many of the *sutras* originated centuries after the historical Buddha, and their sources are unknown. A *shastra* is a document written by someone who is known by name. A *shastra* seeks to be more systematic than the *sutras*. They are in effect commentaries upon the canonical record.

The extant scriptures of Buddhism now form three large collections. First, the Pali Tripitaka contains the scriptures of the Theravādins, although some subdivisions of the sect possess scriptures that are partly preserved in Sanskrit and Chinese. Second, the Chinese Tripitaka varies in the content of its canon and has been more flexibly conceived as a canon. The latest Japanese edition accounts for 2,184 works in 55 volumes of about 1,000 pages each. A record of the Chinese Tripitaka of the sixth century A.D., however, mentions 2,113 works, of which only 276 are still in existence. Third, the Tibetan Kanjur and Tanjur comprise another collection. The Kanjur, composed of about 100 volumes, is a collection of the *sutras*. About 225 volumes comprise the Tanjur, which consists of commentaries and *shastras*.

In addition to the sacred scriptures, Buddhism also cherishes a variety of other documents, such as commentaries on the Tripitaka written by persons of greater and lesser ability in a variety of times and places.

Buddhism lacks the strong sense of canonicity that characterizes the Semitic religions: Judaism, Christianity, and Islam. Its sacred scriptures as a whole are not considered to be the revealed word of God. Their ultimate source of sanctity lies in the fact that some of them reflect the words and teachings of the historical Buddha. An exception to this general rule may be found in Ceylon, where certain Buddhists are biblio-centered even to the extent of worshiping the traditional words of the Buddha.

A difference in attitude exists between the Theravada and the Mahayana Buddhists as to the authority of the scriptures. The Theravada Buddhists are more inclined to respect the Pali Tripitaka as their final authority. They possess a greater sense of the contents of the canon, rejecting some Mahayana scriptures as later creations which do not reflect the original teachings of the Buddha. Mahayana Buddhists in general have looked upon the Buddhist scriptures as the chief source of knowledge, although their canon differs from Theravada Buddhists. The Zen sect within Mahayana Buddhism, however, does not rely upon the scriptures. It believes that it is possible for the believer to obtain direct insight into the ultimate nature of change. One of its famous declarations is that only silence avoids violating the truth. Yet Zen does not reject the scriptures.

One of Zen Buddhism's most revered scriptures is the Saddharma Punkarika Sutra or Lotus Sutra. This was probably compiled in northwestern India around the first century A.D. Later it made its way in various translations throughout the Mahayana Buddhist world. Today the Lotus Sutra is known on a world-wide basis. The Sutra consists of twenty-eight chapters; the first fourteen discuss the nature of man, while the second half deals with the nature of the Buddha. The emphasis in the first part is upon the potentialities of man, who is capable of the greatest evil and the greatest good. If he chooses to stress the evil aspect of his nature he can reach the lowest depths of degredation. But if he chooses the good, he is capable of becoming a powerfully spiritual being who may even approach Buddhahood.

The second half of the Sutra teaches that the historical Buddha is the same as the eternal truth and goodness to which Buddhism points. As no separation exists between the original Buddha and the goal of life, so the world must be viewed as a unity of experience. Evil and good do exist in the world. The ordinary person is well aware of this duality. But an enlightened one, like the Buddha himself, is able to view them in terms of their totality, with desire dispossessed. Then the person who sees reality as through the eyes of the Buddha becomes truly free and experiences no frustration. The inner world of the believer has changed, even though the superficial outer world has not changed. This is the teaching of the Lotus Sutra.

In the main the attitudes of Buddhists are formed by their membership within the sectarian subdivisions of Buddhism. Although

there are two main schools of Buddhist thought, these in turn are
further divided into many dozens or hundreds of smaller groups.
Each has its own special way of viewing Buddhism's sacred scriptures.

TEACHINGS

We have seen that all Buddhism can be divided into the two
major schools: Theravada and Mahayana. Such classification is a
common practice among Buddhists, although some authorities sug-
gest other divisions. Usually these are so impressed with the importance of a subgroup that they succumb to the temptation of making an essentially minor school into a major one. General agreement,
however, supports two major schools.

Theravada Buddhism is clearly the older of the two forms. It is
the orthodox tradition, maintained in Pali, whose teachings and
practices in the main can be traced back to the earliest period of
Buddhism. But the original form of Buddhism was not able to maintain the original form of the *sangha*, and many divergent or heretical
schools arose to challenge the orthodox Theravada. A significant
break with the Theravada tradition took place at the time of the
Second Great Council, when the Mahasanghika school, a precursor
of Mahayana Buddhism, was established. Sarvastivada, the second
major group to break with Theravada Buddhism, differed in only
a few details, but over a period of time its followers gave support to
Mahayana Buddhism.

For a long time Theravada and Mahayana Buddhism existed side
by side in many places. But gradually Theravada became dominant
in southeast Asia, while Mahayana held forth in the northeast.

The names of the schools call for consideration. *Theravada* connotes the Way of the Elders. Sometimes it is called by its followers
the Old Wisdom School. *Mahayana* means the Great Career or the
Great Vehicle. A "vehicle" in this context is a form or instrument
of communication. Followers of Mahayana Buddhism and others
have spoken of Theravada Buddhism as *Hinayana*. This term is
widely found in the literature on Buddhism and suggests the Lesser,

Inferior, or Low Vehicle. Originally Hinayana was a term of abuse, and even today it does not fully escape a negative connotation. Mahayanaists often refer to members of Theravada as the Disciples. Sometimes, too, Mahayana is translated as "the Big Ferryboat" and Hinayana as "the Little Ferryboat." Mahayana is the ferry in which all may ride; Hinayana is the way of the lonely ones, those who are a light unto themselves or who steer their own course to fulfillment.

Theravada and Mahayana Buddhism presented different and sometimes even contrasting appeals. Theravada is not strong in its philosophical outreach. It left many areas of intellectual inquiry open to the more abstract Mahayana. Similarly Theravada ethics are stern; extreme self-denial is required of its followers. Mahayana, on the other hand, provides more room for worldly enjoyment. Thus it may be questioned whether Theravada is the type of religion that would appeal to great masses of people in its purified form. Like ascetic Jainism, it attracts truly heroic persons—such as Mahavira and the Buddha.

The teaching in Mahayana Buddhism on the Bodhisattvas illustrates the more liberal religious position it has taken historically. In Theravada the term Bodhisattva refers to a person who is on the threshold of consecration into Buddhahood. Thus the Buddha was a Bodhisattva before his enlightenment under the Tree of Knowledge. Mahayana, however, employs the term to designate those persons who are sublimely indifferent. These do not seek to cross the threshold of consecration; they remain on it. They do not experience the real or true enlightenment (*samyaksambodhi*) of the Buddha and so on to final extinction of the self (*parinirvana*). They stop at the threshold, and by doing so transcend the realms both of existence and of nonexistence. They remain in existence to point the way to nonexistence to others. Being perpetually on the brink of nonexistence they are able to communicate the meaning of *nirvana* to earthbound persons in a direct and objective way.

In Mahayana Buddhism the attainment of the state of the Bodhisattva is not given merely to a few. Followers of the Mahayana school believe that many Bodhisattvas exist. The state is positively available to the many, and there is no single earthly configuration

which the Bodhisattvas must necessarily assume. Their characters
are varied. Such variation supports the teaching of Mahayana Buddhism that there is no limitation to the number of ways in which
the essential form of Buddhahood may be expressed in human personality. Some Bodhisattvas excel in wisdom. Their main task is
that of overcoming the illusion of subject and object. Other Bodhisattvas exemplify mercy. They find a blissful life in serving others.
Other Bodhisattvas take other forms. But there is one, according to
Mahayana belief, who has not yet appeared on earth. He is Maitreyi
Bodhisattva. He presently lives in heaven, but faithful Buddhists
believe that he will assume human form in the future when the
teachings of the Buddha die. At that time this Benevolent One
(*Maitreyi*) will provide a fresh impetus to others to revive the agelong teachings of the Buddha.

As for the sectarian groups into which the two major schools have
been divided in the long course of their development, those within
Theravada are minor in importance. They primarily reflect the different national and cultural setings in which Theravada exists. The
Pali Tripitika is a strong force for unity throughout the Buddhism
of southeast Asia.

Mahayana Buddhism, however, is characterized by a number of
quite distinctive sects. These reflect the development of very different rituals, philosophies, and scriptures. Their development within
the contexts of national cultures is also significant. Actually there
are dozens of major sectarian groupings within Buddhism, both
today and in the past. Hundreds of divisions of lesser importance
make Buddhism a highly fragmented religion. A full account of
even a few would require several volumes the size of the present
one. Thus, no attempt will be made here to list or comment upon
more than three: Yogacara, Tibetan Buddhism or Lamaism, and
Zen. These are not representative of Buddhism as a whole; they
merely illustrate some of the existing subforms of Buddhism.

The Yogacara school of Mahayana Buddhism was founded by
two brothers, Asanga and Vasubandhu, traders of northwest India,
about 400 A.D. The brothers were philosophically gifted and developed a detailed system of speculation which laid great stress upon

logic. Members of this school were highly skilled in argumentation. They enjoyed debate, especially with Hindus. Through such exercises they developed highly complicated systems of abstract thought based upon Buddhism. They were not restricted in their efforts to the orthodoxy of the Theravada tradition, but were encouraged in the spirit of Mahayana to establish modes of thinking which were self-justifying on logical grounds.

The Yogacara school deviated from other Buddhist schools on several points. For example, it speaks of *nirvana* in essentially positive terms, calling it Mind-Only. *Nirvana* elsewhere in Buddhism has been described partially in negative terms: it is that which is not. The Yogacara school supports its positive conception of *nirvana* with a dualistic view of reality. The mind is good; the body and all matter are evil. Through the use of yogic methods the devout Buddhist is able to suppress the negative encroachments of matter and attain a state of *nirvana* in which mind-only exists.

A correlative concept in the Yogacara school is Store-consciousness. This idea is almost unintelligible, but it may signify those impressions from the whole of past experience which are stored in consciousness for present and future use. Store-consciousness apparently is not a simple equivalent for the memory, soul, or self of the individual. It is a more mystically grounded and inexpressible attribute of the human personality.

The Yogacara school also emphasizes the doctrine of the three bodies of the Buddha: the Dharma-body, the Enjoyment-body, and the Apparitional-body. The Dharma-body is the Buddha as the Absolute. This has a single and superior existence to the other two. The other two bodies emanate from the Dharma-body and are supported by it. The Enjoyment-body of the Buddha consists of the various Bodhisattvas. These express the pure Buddha in various ways. The Apparitional-body consists of those persons of a fictitious or magical nature whose motions of practicing austerities, descending from heaven, winning enlightenment, teaching disciples, and dying on earth lead persons of little insight to grasp the meaning of Buddhism. The reliance of members of this school upon the numerous forms of *yoga,* as the name implies, is paramount.

The Yogacara school disappeared from India about 1100 A.D. Still somewhat active in Tibet, in China and Japan it attracted many followers. Today it has survived as one of the smaller Japanese sects. It has forty-four temples and monasteries and about 700 priests.

Another and quite different form of Mahayana Buddhism exists in Tibet. This form is sometimes called Lamaism, a term meaning the "superior one," which is reserved for the heads of monasteries and high dignitaries, Lamas being the high priests of Tibetan Buddhism. Below them are the Ge-tsu or deacons and the Gen-ye or novices. Below these three groups come the Ge-snen or lay adherents, who are similar in status to laymen in Theravada Buddhism. In Tibet's capital city of Lhasa was the Grand Lama, the Dalai Lama. Now he and some followers are in exile in India. "Dalai" means "the sea," that is, that which is profound and measureless. The Dalai Lama acquired his title in the sixteenth century when his presumed predecessor journeyed to Mongolia in disguise and revived Buddhism there. As a consequence, the Tibetan form of Buddhism is known throughout Mongolia. Some scholars, moreover, consider Lamaism a major form of Buddhism—on a par with the Theravada and Mahayana forms. In this book, however, we are viewing it as a subform of Mahayana Buddhism.

Buddhism was never able to establish itself in a pure form in Tibet. It found there an animistic religion, and became intertwined with it and with a form of Hinduism which is called Tantrism. Tantrism is a Hindu teaching based on manuals (*tantras*) and devoted to that energy which is inherent in everything (*shakti*). It holds that the passions which keep a person from the blessed state of *nirvana* can be explored by their full exercise. Thus the craving for food is destroyed by overindulgence. So with the other passions, including sexuality. Tantrism was merged with Buddhism to form a combination of both which today is called Buddhism in Tibet and elsewhere.

A variety of magical recitations and performances is required in Tibetan Buddhism. There Buddhists believe that diseases and other misfortunes are due primarily to the influence of demonic powers, and that certain words have the power to drive the demons out or to neutralize them. Thus the recitation of spells (*mantra*) has become a much-elaborated feature of the religion, and a highly specialized priesthood has this special responsibility. Ritual gestures are also important in Lamaism. Many of these are apparent from the Tibetan statues of Buddhas and Bodhisattvas. Certain ritual movements, sometimes involving bodies, minds, and speech, create trance-like states for protection from evil. Tibetan Buddhists use revolving barrels of various sizes containing books of sacred writing and written prayers inside them. These have sometimes been erroneously called prayer-wheels. The Tibetans turn the prayer barrels as an act of devotion, either manually or automatically through the force of a running stream.

Tibetan Buddhists distinguish between a left-handed and a right-handed *tantra*. Left-handed observers are basically devoted to the female principle in the universe, while the right-handed observers claim that the male principle is more important. The left-handed believers are prone to the worship of Shakti as the female deity with whom the male deities are united in sexual embrace and from which the male deities receive their power, by the presence of large numbers of terrifying deities and demons, and by the inclusion of sexual intercourse among the other practices necessary for salvation.

Another and quite different form of Mahayana Buddhism has received increasing attention in the West. Zen Buddhism is difficult to place properly even within Mahayana Buddhism, because it ruthlessly denies the importance of all Buddhist teachings as essential to the attainment of enlightenment. In Zen everything can be used for devotional purposes, but nothing is necessary or even important. Concepts of God, soul, or salvation, the use of scriptures, ritual, or vow, and other elements of religion may aid the follower of Zen, but none of these is necessary. Commonly they are even scorned as having no essential value. Because Zen is so highly negative toward the traditional elements of Buddhism it is not always classified either within or outside of Buddhism as a form or heresy of that religion. It is largely found today in China and Japan, where it has appealed especially to members of the military class.

The primary purpose of Zen Buddhism is to achieve immediate

and direct knowledge. The Zen Buddhist says that everyone, even the expert, knows only about things. Everyone in ordinary living is restrained by concepts or mental images and habitual practices from piercing directly into the core of meaning. All words are severely limited. None exhausts the utter meaning of its reference. Even the intellect itself is an inferior agent in attaining immediate and direct knowledge. The intellect in its ordinary activities is burdened with words, concepts, and emotions which are also part of ordinary experience.

Zen offers the believer a means of transcending thinking. It claims that it is possible through the use of certain techniques to jump from second-hand to immediate and direct experience. The use of Zen techniques leads to *satori,* the Zen name for enlightenment. The *mondo* is a technique in which rapid questioning and answering between master and pupil is so speeded up that the ordinary process of thought is suddenly transcended. The *koan* signifies a word or phrase that is insoluble to the intellect. Neither the *mondo* nor the *koan* has any meaning for the rational mind. The *koan,* to supply illustrations, teaches the rational mind to accept nonsense. When two hands are clapped together they make a noise, but what is the sound of one hand clapping? To what is the One reduced if all things are reducible to the One? Or, what would a man say if he were asked the meaning of Zen while hanging over a precipice by his teeth with his hands and feet immobilized?

The *koan* form of technique in Zen Buddhism shows that nonsense is the product of reasoning and logic. Zen laughs at such reasoning and logic. According to Zen all thoughts or emotions which shape the ordinary ways by which men seize essential knowledge must be shattered, including all formulas, phrases, dogmas, codes, schools, systems of thought, philosophy, and isms, including Buddhism. The result of the application of Zen techniques is the attainment of the goal of *satori.*

But *satori* is a distinctive form of Buddhist enlightenment. It is a condition of consciousness in which distractions and opposites are balanced by intuitive or mystical experience. The person who attains *satori* is not in or out of the body; he is not in or out of the world.

He is able, however, to see and appreciate the whole as well as its parts in their proper proportion. *Satori* is the Absolute Moment. The practical consequence of achieving some degree of *satori* is the possession of clarity of mind, inner certainty of purpose, and an understanding of the way by which these values may be increased. The practice of Zen leads to further development of the practitioner until finally it may be said that a person is markedly changed or reborn.

These three subforms of Mahayana Buddhism—Yogacara, Tibetan Buddhism or Lamaism, and Zen—comprise only three particular expressions. Many more exist. But these provide some insight into the complex development and character of one of the major schools of Buddhism.

God

Because of the highly diverse character of Buddhism it is probably impossible to provide a comprehensive and balanced description of its teachings on God, the person, and society. Each of the major schools of thought and their many subdivisions hold special views on each of these themes. Yet by stressing the original teachings of the Buddha, insofar as they are known, some notion may be secured of the religion's teachings. A cautious spirit will prevent acceptance of any particular teaching as representing the whole of Buddhism.

Original Buddhism and many of its later schools clearly teach that there is no God in the traditional meaning. Buddhism is more accurately described as atheist than as theist. Buddha refrained from teaching the doctrine of God, and his immediate followers, aside from the deification of the Buddha, failed to develop any teaching on the subject.

Similarly there has been no doctrine of creation, as this concept is commonly understood. There is no ultimate origin; there is only cause and effect, which is derived infinitely from the past. The universe has evolved, but its evolution is based upon the materials of a previous universe. So, in the future, other universes will come into being. Existence, moreover, cannot be described in either/or terms. According to Buddhist thought there are thirty-seven planes of existence, the four lowest of which are known as the Four States of Unhappiness. Just above these are the Seven Happy States in which human beings exist. Above these are the six planes of the lower heavenly beings. All seventeen planes are based upon desire, but above them are twenty planes of existence of the higher heavenly beings. These do not know desire.

In another classification of the attributes of all physical and mental phenomena, including man, the Buddha spoke of five "aggregates" (*skandhas*). These five groups of existence are: corporeality, feeling, perception, mental formations, and consciousness. Corporeality or matter is further analyzed into four essential elements: extension, cohesion, heat, and motion. Since all existence involves a changing combination of the five aggregates, a principle is sought in Buddhism to regulate the change. The principle is *karma*. *Karma* is the order of cause and effect in action, including all good and bad actions whether they are intentional or not. The doctrine of *karma* teaches that every action in a moment of time is highly influenced by every other action of the past. Yet the present is not simply determined by the past. Action in the present, moreover, is highly significant because it tends to influence future actions. Although *karma* operates impersonally and its power lies beyond human control, an understanding of it gives power. As a believer practices the law of the good *karma* he is able to direct his own future as well as that of others. By so doing he helps himself and others to attain the universal goal of *nirvana*.

Despite the positive aspects of the doctrine of *karma*, the Buddha was not particularly optimistic about the ability of the believer to induce positive change. All existence is painful and calls upon the individual to denounce any naïvely-held sense of power regarding the possibility of overcoming himself and the world. The Buddha indicated that this painfulness has three aspects: impermanence (*anicca*), the ultimate unreality of the self (*anatta*), and suffering or sorrow (*dukkha*). It is the painfulness of existence that encourages the Buddhist to seek *nirvana*, that state of blessedness which releases the person from suffering, the unreality of the self, and transitoriness.

The Person

The teachings of Buddhism regarding the person begin with the Buddha's sermon in the Deer Park at Benares to the five ascetics. On that occasion he gave his hearers and the world the Four Noble Truths. First, the Buddha taught the Noble Truth of Desire (*tanha*) or Suffering (*dukkha*). He declared that birth, decay, illness, and death are suffering. The presence of hated objects is suffering. Suffering is likewise caused when the person is separated from objects he loves. Not to obtain what is desired is also suffering. Even to cling to existence, by the means of the five *skandhas*, is suffering.

Second, Buddha taught the Noble Truth of the Origin of Suffering. He declared that suffering is caused by a threefold desire or thirst: the thirst for pleasure, the thirst for existence, and the thirst for prosperity. These lead to rebirth rather than to a state of enlightenment.

Third, the Buddha taught the Noble Truth of the Extinction of Suffering. He declared that the elimination of desire will remove the cause of suffering. Every passion must be destroyed.

The last Noble Truth, according to the Buddha, leads to the Noble Eightfold Path. This will be presented in serial fashion. First, right understanding (*samma ditthi*) refers to a belief in the Noble Truths, the nature of the self and the law of *karma*, and other elements in the belief system of Buddhism. Second, right attitude of mind (*samma sankappa*) signifies the need for proper love of others, the willingness to harm no living thing and to possess a generally constructive stance toward life. Third, right speech (*samma vacha*) involves the conscious control of words so that the language of the believer is courteous, considerate, and true. Even silence can be right speech. Fourth, right action (*samma kammanta*) means that all action, whether positive or negative, is meaningful. In Buddhism five negative precepts (*panchas silas*) are taught. The believer is called upon to abstain from killing, stealing, sensuality, lying, and the use of intoxicating liquors or drugs. Right action, however, is positive action; it is beneficial.

Fifth, right livelihood (*samma ajiva*) calls upon the believer to follow a trade or occupation which is in harmony with the Noble Eightfold Path. Sixth, right effort (*samma vayama*) indicates that the Buddhist cannot be apathetic about his attainment of *nirvana*. He must depend upon his own constant efforts. *Nirvana* is not a collective state; it can only be won by individuals. Four types of right effort have been enunciated: to prevent new evil from entering one's mind, to remove all evil that is there, to develop such good as is in one's mind, and to acquire still more good. Seventh, right recollection (*samma sati*) signifies the beginning of the final stage in which the favored believer is able to control the evolution of his mind. This control is obtained through the art of concentration. Eighth, right meditation (*samma samadhi*) signifies the last phase of the believer's struggle to secure *nirvana*. In this stage the individual is scarcely separated from *nirvana*. He is free from desire, suffering, and rebirth. He is the saintly Buddhist (*arahat*).

By the teachings of the Four Noble Truths and the Noble Eightfold Path, the Buddha laid down for his followers a systematic account of the nature of the human condition and of the ways by which it can be transformed into perfection. Taken together the truths and the path are a sufficiently comprehensive and strenuous prescription for life which makes extended philosophic analysis superfluous. They cover the amount and kind of understanding the individual requires to embark on a practical program for ethical conduct. They also call him to a life of strenuous and supreme meditation.

Taken together, the truths and the path constitute a progressive regimen like the rungs of a ladder whereby the individual may go from stage to stage until he is finally emancipated. The development of the believer by way of the truths and the path is characterized in Buddhist thought as consisting of three stages. First, the believer is to refrain from all evil. Second, he is to do what is good. Third, he must purify his mind.

In the practice of his religion the Buddhist is required to express love. This love or compassion is not simply passive good will. It is a virtue to be offered in the service of one's fellow man. It involves generous-mindedness, kindheartedness, and charitable actions. Buddha employed the figure of speech of a mother's love for her child to explain the quality and depth of the love he preached. Love in this sense is a means of expressing one's solidarity with all mankind and of overcoming the pettiness of a severe individualism.

Buddhism also teaches a belief in reincarnation. Death does not end personal existence. As nothing has ever been created, so nothing can be destroyed. Rebirth is immediate upon death. The physical form of the body is merely the shell of a more essential existence. This existence continues whether in one form or another. The individual through the process of trained contemplation and meditation may be able to recall at least the rough lineaments of a former existence, but whether or not this is so, life, ever obedient to the karmic principle, persists through death.

Nirvana, according to Buddhist teaching, is not the negation of the self. It is indeed a blessed state in which all desires or thirsts are eliminated. No lust, hatred, or ignorance characterizses it. In Pali, nirvana means "no desire." In Sanskrit it means "the blowing out." What is blown out is the flame of craving. Actually nirvana is a logically inexpressible concept. The most that can be said about it is that it is, for any positive assertion about it leads to misunderstandings. On the other hand, it is very easy and proper to say what it is not. Almost any characterization of it can be logically denied. It is a state of existence which goes beyond the usual limits of reality.

Buddhism's teaching regarding the self is similar to that for nirvana. Throughout the long course of Buddhism's history the principle of the nonego (anatta) has been taught. The doctrine of the nonego signifies that the individual ego is a delusion. The Buddha refrained from assuming that the self partakes of a metaphysical substance. He denied that there is a single existence or attribute of which the soul is an expression. He taught that a highly changeable and impermanent group of elements make up the self. These are five in number: the body, the feelings, conceptual knowledge based on sense-perception, the instincts and the subconscious, and consciousness in the form of human reason. All of these together make up the individual. As long as they function harmoniously the individual is unified and existent. If one or more changes radically, the nature of the self similarly changes.

The Buddha's doctrine of the nonego seems to apply his cosmic atheism to the individual. It is not clear, moreover, how a denial of self can be harmonized with such other doctrines in Buddhism as *karma* and rebirth.

Society

Buddhism is primarily a religion for individuals. It does not contain systematic teachings regarding society. Insofar as it possesses an atttude toward society, it may be said to be negative. Society does not support the individual in his quest for *nirvana*. Contrariwise, it is a principle source of desire and suffering. In fact, the monastic life is viewed in Buddhism as the superior state. The religion permits laymen to be Buddhists and describes a series of five prohibitions for them: do not kill, steal, commit adultery, lie, or drink intoxicants. But whether layman or monk, the individual is encouraged to lead a quiet, individualistic life. Thus Buddhism does not possess any organized program of social amelioration. It teaches individual salvation.

Of course, it enjoins the individual to possess right attitudes, to love others, and to maximize the potential of the karmic opportunity. All these and other elements require the believer to act constructively as a person in his social relationships. In this sense Buddhism has had a social impact.

Socially in India the Buddha protested against the caste system. For a long period of time Buddhism was one of the principal forces which loosened the hold of this Hindu teaching. The formation of the order (*sangha*) into which members of all castes and kinds were inducted almost dealt a death blow to caste. For centuries Buddhism was an anticaste power in Indian life. In many parts of Asia to which Buddhism later went, however, there was no caste system against which to protest. But there were social differentiations, some of which were sharp and oppressive. Wherever Buddhism spread it provided a concrete social form for the equalization of all persons in the *sangha*.

The *sangha* has performed two essential functions in society. First, it has been the agency whereby piety and reflection in the Buddhist manner is given honor and form. Thus, members of the religious order are testimonies to the higher version of life which was introduced by the Buddha. Second, the *sangha* has been the agency whereby society through its support acknowledges the basic principles upon which its hope ultimately rests for peace and security. These two functions point to the fact that there is a real connection between the *sangha* and society. Society is undergirded by the *sangha*. The inescapable presence of the monks in society has a marked effect. At the same time, society support the *sangha* and in that support is molded in character and outlook.

Although the *sangha* has been an integrating force among Buddhists and a democratizing influence in society generally, it was actually composed of four groups of people: monks (*bhikkhus*), nuns (*bhikkhunis*), male lay adherents (*upasakas*), and female lay adherents (*upasikas*). Originally it had no religious head. Groups of monks were under the guidance of an elderly member of their own group who expressed its authority. The monks and nuns did gather occasionally to recite the rules of conduct or engage in study. Nuns lived apart from the monks except when they came together for official activities. In time, however, the nature of the *sangha*, especially in Mahayana countries, changed considerably. Images, signs, ceremonies, festivals, and worship were introduced, sometimes in elaborate forms. The informal and direct communion of the early *sangha* gave way to the organization of the institutional *sangha* with its complicated appurtenances. Spiritual, mythological, and even magical elements were added to the simple religion of the Buddha and his disciples. Buddhism had come of age.

We have noted already that this religion, despite its emphasis upon individual responsibility and salvation, appealed to the rulers of nations. Asoka and Kanishka among others in India, Songstan-Gampo in Tibet, and Shotoku Taishi in Japan not only were Buddhists, but used governmental power to extend the faith. In several periods of its life and in a number of countries Buddhism has become the state religion. Thus there appears to be no necessary incompatibility between the religion and the proper social functions of the state.

Buddhism has never had a centralized system of organization. Its history is characterized by extreme diversity of ecclesiastical structure. It possesses no world council in which the schools and their subdivisions are in direct and continuous communication with each other. There is also no one person in whom supreme religious authority is invested as in the Pope in Roman Catholic Christianity. Buddhism, however, despite its relatively loose organization, has developed into a major religious system. It has molded the life of much of Asia. It was India's contribution to the world.

ANNOTATED BIBLIOGRAPHY
ON BUDDHISM

1 ALLEN, G. F. *The Buddha's Philosophy: Selections from the Pali Canon and an Introductory Essay.* London: George Allen & Unwin, 1959. A description of the Buddha and his teachings.

*2 BAHM, A. J. *Philosophy of the Buddha.* New York: Collier Books, 1962. A fresh view of the subject, based on Buddhist scriptures.

*3 BARRETT, WILLIAM, ed. *Zen Buddhism: Selected Writings of D. T. Suzuki.* Garden City, N. Y.: Doubleday, Anchor Books, 1956. An introduction to the history and spirit of Zen Buddhism as seen through the eyes of Zen's late chief exponent.

*4 BURTT, EDWIN, ed. and comment. *The Teachings of the Compassionate Buddha: Early Discourses, The Dhammapada, and Later Basic Writings.* New York: Mentor Books, New American Library, 1955. A selection of important scriptures with helpful introduction and notes.

*5 CONZE, EDWARD. *Buddhism: Its Essence and Development.* New York: Harper Torchbooks, 1959. A reliable, general, yet brief book on the nature and history of Buddhism.

6 ELLIOT, CHARLES. *Hinduism and Buddhism,* rev. ed. London: Routledge & Kegan Paul, 1954. A dependable analysis of the similarities and differences of the two religions.

*7 HAMILTON, CLARENCE. *Buddhism: A Religion of Infinite Compassion.* New York: Bobbs-Merrill Co., 1952. Selections from Buddhist literature.

*8 HUMPHREYS, CHRISTMAS. *Buddhism.* Baltimore: Penguin Books, 1951. A sympathetic scholar presents the history, development, and present-day teachings of the various schools of Buddhism.

*9 ————. *Zen Buddhism.* New York The Macmillan Co., 1962. A popular survey of the school, including its nature, history, techniques, and fruits.

* Paperback.

*10 LATOURETTE, KENNETH. *Introducing Buddhism.* New York: Friendship Press, 1956. A brief account for the beginner.

11 MORGAN, KENNETH, ed. *The Path of the Buddha: Buddhism Interpreted by Buddhists.* New York: Ronald Press, 1956. A vivid account of Buddhism, its nature, history, beliefs, and practices, by practicing Buddhists.

12 PERCHERON, MAURICE. *The Marvelous Life of the Buddha.* New York: St. Martin's Press, 1960. An artistically valuable interpretation.

13 PRATT, JAMES. *The Pilgrimage of Buddhism and a Buddhist Pilgrimage.* New York: The Macmillan Co., 1928. A large and older book which combines many details of Buddhist religion and culture with philosophical reasoning.

14 SUZUKI, BEATRICE. *Mahayana Buddhism.* New York: The Macmillan Co., 1959. A good source for the beginner.

*15 SUZUKI, DAISETZ TEITARO. *Mysticism: Christian and Buddhist, The Eastern and the Western Way.* New York: Collier Books, 1962. This book shows how Zen and Shin Buddhism of the East and the Christian mysticism of Meister Eckhart meet on common ground.

16 WALTERS, JOHN. *The Essence of Buddhism.* New York: Crowell-Collier Pub. Co., 1961. An attempt to show the relevance of Buddhism for modern life.

Sikhism

A GLOSSARY OF SIKH TERMS

Adi Granth	The first or primary scriptures of Sikhism.
Akal	The timeless, a term for God.
Akalis	A major Sikh sect, meaning "immortals"; also known as Nihangs or Shahidis.
Allah	The Muslim term for God.
Amritsar	The central Sikh shrine, the "pool of immortality."
Avatar	A descent of deity or incarnation.
Bawan-akhari	A lengthy acrostic in the Sikh sacred scriptures, the Fifty-two.
Bhagat	A devoted disciple or saint.
Darbar	A court.
Deva	A god.
Granth Sahib	The Sikh Bible, the "Lord Book."
Gurdwara	A village shrine.
Guru	A spiritual teacher who instructs disciples; a name also for God.
Gyani	One who expounds religious texts.
Islam	"Submission," the name of the religion founded by Muhammed.
Janamsakhis	Sikh birth stories and records.
Japji	A hymn, a morning declaration to God.
Kachk	The requirement that short drawers be worn.
Kangha	The requirement that a comb be worn in the hair.
Kara	The requirement that a steel or iron bracelet be worn.
Karma	The principle of causality in moral experience.
Kes	The requirement of long hair on the head and chin.
Khalsa	A special order of Sikhs.
Khanda	The requirement that a two-edged dagger be carried.
Khatri	A subdivision of the Kshatriya or warrior caste.
Khudda	The glorious, a name for the deity in Islam.

171

Kshatriya	A member of the warrior or second highest caste in India.
Kukkas	Required code of conduct, consisting of five prescriptions.
Mahdi	The title of an expected spiritual or temporal ruler in Islam.
Maya	Illusion.
Misl	Like, equal.
Nanakpanthis	A major Sikh sect, followers of Nanak's path.
Nihangs	A major Sikh sect, meaning "reckless"; also known as Akalis or Shahidis.
Nirdun	Absolute, an attribute of deity.
Nirmalis	A major Sikh sect, who led ascetic lives.
Nirvana	Enlightment, freedom from self, the end of selfiish desires, the state of salvation.
Panthis	The path, connoting the way and teachings of a Guru.
Pathshala	A local elementary school.
Safa	A white sheet or outer garment.
Sangha	A religious order as in Jainism and Buddhism.
Sat Nam	The true name, a name for God.
Sati	Widow-burning, sometimes spelled "suttee."
Satun	Personal, an attribute of deity.
Sewapanthis	A major Sikh sect, who laid stress on impartial service.
Shadi	Marriage.
Shahidis	A major Sikh sect, meaning "martyrs"; also known as Akalis or Nihangs.
Shiksha	Instruction, disciple or learner.
Singh	A member of the Khalsa, a Sikh sect, "lion."
Suf	A coarse garb, characteristically worn by Sufis.
Sukhmani	The Peace-Jewel, a section of the Sikh sacred scriptures.
Takhallus	The use by writers of the Sikh sacred scriptures of the name of Nanak as a *nom-de-plume*.
Udas	A feeling of sorrow.
Udasis	A major Sikh sect, founded by Nanak's son and based on a sorrowful view of society.

V

SIKHISM

INTRODUCTION

SIKHISM IS CHRONOLOGICALLY the fourth major religion to have arisen in India. There have been only a few periods in the advanced societies of human history in which new religions have emerged. Several, such as Hinduism and Shintoism, probably derive from prehistoric times. So distant in years are their beginnings that little today can be said with accuracy about the conditions that brought them forth. The origins of Zoroastrianism date, according to some scholars, from the seventh century B.C., but the largest number of the living religions were born in the sixth century B.C.: Buddhism, Confucianism, Jainism, and Taoism. This general period was obviously one of the greatest creative eras in religion known to man.

Several religions are exceptions to the pattern. Judaism may be said to date back to the giving of the Law at Sinai, possibly in the thirteenth century B.C. Christianity also stands alone in the time of its inception. By the time Christianity came upon the scene eight other religions had had a long and varied history. Islam and Sikhism were established after Christianity. Islam began in the seventh century A.D. and bore a direct relationship to both Judaism and Christianity. Sikhism originated in the fifteen century A.D. and is intimately related to both Hinduism and Islam.

Sikhism, like Islam, did not begin its life in the distant mists of human history, but in the light of historical consciousness. To some extent Christianity, Jainism, and Buddhism are also open to more precise historical examination than Hinduism. All these later religions, moreover, may be called responses to already existing and

173

somewhat defined religious life. Yet, the task of separating fact from legend remains with all the religions. Despite its recency, Sikhism, especially in the life of its founder, presents formidable problems of isolating truth from fiction.

Its founder, Nanak (1469-1538 A.D.), was contemporaneous with Martin Luther. He succeeded in establishing an independent religion, with its own distinctive doctrines, a new set of scriptures, and a fresh and distinctive theology. Luther, on the other hand, did not break with Christianity. He launched a reform movement in relation to the major expression of Christianity in his time: the Roman Catholic Church.

Nanak is unique in the history of religions. He sought not merely to reform a religion, but to fuse together two of the great religions of his own land and period: Hinduism and Islam. His syncretic effort was a success. From Islam mainly he took a severe monotheism; much of the rest of Sikhism came from Hinduism. Nanak himself did not originate any new doctrine or practice. As founder of a religion he is noted for two accomplishments. First, he selected teachings of Hinduism and Islam that together formed a new system of belief and practice. Second, he gave emphasis to his selections by his life and teachings. These two elements—selection and personal emphasis—were the primary bases for the formation of the Sikh faith.

The religion derives its name from the Sanskrit word for disciple or learner (*shiksha*): the Sikh is one who is under instruction in the religious way of life established by Nanak.

Sikhism illustrates a possible response on the part of religions that are related geographically and theologically to other religions. Nanak was a Hindu; his disciples were Hindus or Muslims, for the most part. Both Hinduism and Islam flourished in India in Nanak's time. His religion is syncretic; that is, represents a deliberate and conscious effort to integrate religions already on the scene. Sikhism undoubtedly sought at first to displace both Hinduism and Islam, but this did not happen. In fact, the history of religion teaches that individuals may be converted from one religion to another, but religions as such are never converted. The high aim of Sikhism in its original period was not realized, and Hinduism and Islam maintained their autonomy.

As in the Punjab of India, where the Sikh religion first saw light, major and living religions exist and work side by side nowadays in many of the advanced societies of the world. There is scarcely a nation where there is not more than one religious option. Sikhism, therefore, illustrates one way in which a religion can relate itself to others.

This faith bears the relationship to Islam which traditionally Islam has borne to Christianity and perhaps also to Judaism. Sikhism claimed to be a religion superior to Islam. It occurred historically later, and sought to build upon it. A similar parallelism exists between Islam and Christianity. Islam from the time of its founding has considered itself a new dispensation. It believes that its teachings supersede those of Christianity. It does not hold that they negate those of Christianity; rather, from its own point of view, it has placed religion on an even higher plane. So, too, with Judaism. Islam does not repudiate Judaism. It has been quite willing to recognize the values of the preparatory religious activities of Judaism for the inception and development of Islam. Christians and Jews, of course, do not accept these claims of Islam, but assume that their own religions represent the highest available forms. Similarly, Muslims do not consider Sikhism to be a superior religion, but view it as an unfortunate heresy.

Sikhism has been more widely accepted by Hindus than by Muslims, possibly because Hinduism is much more tolerant of other religions than Islam. The latter, in the Semitic tradition, possesses a fierce attachment to the truth as it conceives it to be. This attribute also is characteristic of Judaism and Christianity. Hinduism, however, has always been more willing and able to accept what others would call heresies. It is rather open-minded toward views even diametrically opposed to those taught in the Vedic religion.

Observers are certain that Sikhism is not a sectarian offshoot of Islam. The two religions are clearly distinct and in times past have even militarily opposed each other. But it has been remarked that Sikhism might be considered a Hindu sect. This classification is not of the Sikhs' making. It is based upon an essentially Hindu view of religion, which in its broadmindedness is able to encompass Sikhism.

Sikhism originated and continues to be found predominantly in the Punjab, a province of northwest India. The Sikhs today are found on the broad, alluvial plane along the Sutlej River, a chief tributary to the Indus River network whose waters ultimately flow into the Arabian Sea. Sikhs are also found, although sparsely, in the Central Provinces and Berar, and in Orissa in India, and lastly in Baluchistan and Sind in postpartition Pakistan. Because of the compatibility of their political interests with the British, the Sikhs are found in military and police service in such farflung places as Aden, Durban, Hong Kong, Penang, Singapore, and Shanghai. They are known throughout India as expert taxi men and bodyguards. Ordinarily, however, they are not an urban people. Originally their tasks were pastoral and agricultural. In their native lands they continue today mainly in these occupations, although some have engaged in trading and the manufacture of textiles.

The Sikhs suffered as a consequence of the partitioning of India in 1947. Their home territory was split between what is now Pakistan and India. Amritsar, the most important shrine of the Sikh faith, is in Indian territory. The Sikhs in the period of the partitioning, like their Hindu and Muslim counterparts, became incensed over the division and fought fiercely for their rights. Their native territory, however, continues to be divided, although they have been assured of religious freedom by both Pakistan and India.

In the number of its adherents Sikhism is small, particularly when compared to the other religions of modern India and Pakistan. The 1941 prepartition census indicated the following population division according to religion in India: 255 million Hindus, 92 million Muslims, 25 million tribal religious adherents, 6 million Christians, 6 million Sikhs, 1.5 million Jains, 232 thousand Buddhists, 114 thousand Parsis or followers of Zoroastrianism, and 434 thousand others. The partitioning of British India in 1947, however, brought about a shift of approximately 12 million Hindus and Muslims combined, each moving to the new nation where their religion is dominant.

Today in the Republic of India, Hindus claim 85 per cent of the population, while Muslims claim nearly 10 per cent. There are about 2.3 per cent Christians and something less than 2 per cent of Sikhs in the Republic.

Students of religion in general and Sikhism in particular are not in agreement on the number of Sikhs in the subcontinent. Some estimates run as low as 4 million, while generally Sikh membership is placed at about 6 million. By any of these estimates, however, Sikhism is a relatively small religion, ranking along with Jainism, Zoroastrianism, and even Judaism. The importance of a religion, however, cannot be evaluated on the basis of the number of its adherents. Truth is never up for vote. As a religious system Sikhism is entitled to careful and sensitive description and evaluation in the same manner as the most populous of the living religions.

In the course of its history Sikhism gave birth to a nation. During the period of Guru Gobind Singh (1675-1708 A.D.), the religion was transformed into a militant theocracy. At this time, and as a result of the preceding warfare, the Sikhs became an independent state with Dacca as their capital. Sikhism, however, is not distinctive in this respect. Judaism may also be viewed as a religion that created a nation. Perhaps even the founding of modern Israel is a consequence of Judaism's political implications and aspirations. Similarly Shintoism has greatly contributed to the formation of the national culture of Japan. The Sikhs today, however, are not a nation; they are citizens of Pakistan and India.

Architecturally, too, Sikhism has been creative. Throughout the area af its predominance, it has created houses of worship which are places of great beauty. Sikh shrines in villages and towns are called *gurdwaras* and are readily distinguishable from Hindu temples, Muslim mosques, Christian churches, and other places of worship. *Gurdwara* means a doorway to the Guru or the head of the Sikh religion. The chief Sikh shrine is the Golden Temple or Darbar Sahib located in Amritsar. The Golden Temple of today is the creation of Maharaja Ranjit Singh, a Sikh who came to power in northwest India in the early nineteenth century. The temple is a court (*darbar*) where the Sikh's deity, despite his extreme transcendence, makes himself available to his worshipers. It rises with a gold top from a five-acre, quadrangular pool of water. This is the "pool of immortality" (*amritsar*). This Golden Temple contains a variety of architectural structures of marble, gilded copper plates, and other materials, some of which are inscribed with texts from the Sikh scriptures. It is a center for worship and pilgrimage. Other Sikh shrines reflect the Sikh interest in establishing esthetically attractive places for worship.

FOUNDER

At the time of Nanak's birth (1469 A.D.) Hinduism and Islam were in competition for men's loyalties in the Punjab. Hinduism as usual expressed itself in several forms. The polytheistic religion of the Vedas and the thoughtful Hinduism based upon the Upanishads were found together in the region. In fact, both prior to and during Nanak's time, Hinduism lacked a perennially needed renewal, and its lower or more decadent forms seemed to predominate. Hinduism was further weakened by the fact that it was not politically supported or enforced. The Muslim rulers persecuted Hindus widely and openly, seizing lands and offices, pillaging their temples, and killing many. Although in some instances intermarriage occurred without the requirement that the Hindu partner give up his faith, Hindus were often forcibly enrolled as Muslims. Hinduism was at low tide.

It had, of course, reached this point before. Traditionally, in times of its degeneracy, reformers had arisen who sought to arouse the people to the true meaning of the faith. Some were quickly forgotten as history hastened along. Others succeeded in renewing Hinduism for long periods of time and in influential ways. Nanak was in a sense a reformer of Hinduism, a major reformer. But he was more. The independent religion he sought to establish took important elements from Hinduism, and also included elements of Islam.

However, Islam also suffered from weaknesses. A number of variants or heresies from Islamic orthodoxy existed. The Shiites, for

example, fit this category. They are distinguished within Islam by
their adherence to a line of blood-descent rather than that of
electoral succession to the prophet Muhammad. Although the Shiites
became the predominant form in what is now Iran, they were also an
important force within Indian Islam, and occasionally engaged in
violence against the Sunnis, the orthodox branch of that faith.

Islam also included in Nanak's time another form: Sufism. This
is not so much a sect as it is a band of Islamic mystics. Sufis generally were counted within the orthodox fold. They wore a coarse garb
(*suf*) and distrusted institutional religion. Sufism in India had developed a fundamental stress upon the transcendence of God
(Allah). God—the Sufis' God—was far beyond man, history, or
nature. Yet according to the teaching, it is possible for a human
being to be united with God through mystical experience. With
the teachings of the Sufis, the schismatic presence of the Shiites,
the divided political loyalies among Muslims, and other factors,
Islam was far from united in sixteenth-century northwest India.

A number of earlier religious reformers were instrumental in
shaping Nanak's thinking. Jaidev, for example, posed in the twelfth
century as a Hindu reformer-poet. Repelled by the multifarious
ceremonies and austerities of the Hinduism of his time, he stressed
the importance of the pious repetition of God's name. This emphasis
on the name of God and its repetition came to the fore ultimately
with Nanak.

In the fourteenth century Ramananda, who sought to reform
Hinduism by preaching against the caste system and vegetarianism,
had great influence upon one Kabir (1440-1518 A.D.), a predecessor
of Nanak who was born near Benares, possibly of a Muslim father
and a Hindu mother. Kabir, a disciple of Ramananda, apparently
criticized both Hinduism and Islam; he denounced idolatry as fool-
ish, false, and wrong, and questioned the value of pilgrimages. He
was opposed to Vedic Hinduism as an unworthy form of religion. He
also questioned the validity of the Koran, the Islamic sacred scriptures, and criticized what he held to be an overemphasis on ritualism
in that religion. He considered himself a teacher (*guru*) and not a
god (*deva*). He laid great stress upon the name of God, maintaining

that the name is superior to all gods, including those of Hinduism and Islam; and he taught that pure love of God freed any and all from the laws of *karma* and rebirth. By loving God completely, he said, one is absorbed into the soul of the Absolute. Since they were phrased in the vernacular rather than in Sanskrit, his teachings received a wide hearing. Kabir laid the groundwork for Nanak's life and teachings.

Nanak was born in Talwandi (later known as Rayapur) on the bank of the Ravi River near Lahore, capital of the Punjab. This city had been founded by a Hindu ruler and most of its residents were Hindus. The ruler at the time of Nanak's birth was Rai Bular, originally a Hindu, who along with his father had been converted to Islam, though the Muslims at that time comprised only 10 to 15 per cent of the population. Rai Bular, after his conversion, was tolerant toward Hindus and open to efforts to reconcile the two religions.

Nanak's father, Kalu, was a *khatri*, a designation which places him at the lower end of the warrior (*kshatriya*) caste. He was a village farmer and accountant. Tripta, daughter of Rama, was Nanak's mother, a woman of humble origin. Both Nanak and his sister, Nanki, were probably born in Tripta's parents' home in Talwandi.

Nanak was enrolled at an early age in the local school (*pathshala*). There he studied Hindi and Urdu, important Indian vernaculars. It is said that Sayyid Hasan, a Muslim villager, was strongly attracted to Nanak and helped him in his education. If he was a Shiite, as is supposed, he probably had an important religious influence upon the boy, who was interested in religion from an early age. Nanak disliked any kind of manual labor and refused to follow the vocations of herdsman or storekeeper that his father chose for him. His inclinations drew him toward the Hindu and Islamic sacred writings. His mind was on religion.

Later he entered the second or householder's stage of Hindu life. At perhaps the age of nineteen he took a bride, Sulakhari, from a village near Sultanpur. His brother-in-law successfully persuaded him to live in Sultanpur and to join him in government service as a revenue collector. But he did not make a success either of his marriage or his work. Apparently Nanak and Sulakhari fought regularly, and she went to her own home for extended periods. Even the two families quarreled. Finally Nanak's wife took their two sons, Sri Chand and Lakhmi Das, and went to live permanently in her parental home. Nanak, although he is said to have been diligent and hardworking, was essentially unhappy. He left his job and became a wanderer. He was joined in his search for salvation by Mardana, a Muslim, and a small group of like-minded seekers.

One day Nanak underwent an ecstatic experience which changed the course of his life and ultimately became the foundation for the Sikh religion. On that day, after bathing in the river, he went into the forest. There he was taken in a vision to the very presence of God, who gave him a cup of nectar and then spoke to him saying that he was with Nanak, that Nanak had made him happy along with all those who would follow Nanak. Nanak was charged to go forth into the world and repeat the Divine Name and cause others to do likewise. He was told to abide uncontaminated in the world, to practice the repetition of God's name, charity, ablutions, worship, and meditation. The cup of nectar was the pledge of God's regard for him.

Nanak then adored God by singing a hymn. Tradition says that heaven joined in spontaneously with accompanying music. He is said to have sung the preamble of the Japji, a poetic tribute repeated silently as a morning declaration by all Sikhs. It is a hymn to God—the True, the Creator, devoid of fear and enmity, immortal, unborn, self-existent, great and bountiful—and to the past, present, and future presence of the True One.

Nanak came forth from the forest after three days, went home, and gave all he had to the poor. He donned a simple loincloth and became a religious ascetic. After a day's silence, he declared that he was neither Hindu nor Muslim. By this statement he condemned the popular religions of his time.

His experience in the forest gave him a foundation for teaching a new religion, one which he believed had superseded Hinduism and Islam. He intended it for all those living within the geographic area covered by the two religions, certainly the whole of India, Iran, and the Arabian peninsula.

The story of Nanak's missionary efforts is long and detailed and cannot be fully recounted here. On his travels he took Mardana as his sole companion. Usually he preached by singing hymns while Mardana accompanied him on a rebec, a small stringed instrument. Together they toured north and west India over a period of years, going into the organized centers of Hinduism to preach their new religion. Nanak sought merely to convert a few persons wherever he went, in the belief that God would sustain his efforts through the few and that they in turn would deliver God's message to others. In time, an inner circle was formed. This included Lahna, who at Nanak's death, under the name of Angad, became the head of the Sikh movement; Bala, a follower from Sind; Ram Das, who was called the "old fellow"; and Sri Chand, Nanak's son. The group can scarcely be called more than a small band of disciples (Sikh means "disciple"). Nanak apparently did nothing to establish a religious order. The fact is, he was opposed to institutionalized religion.

In his conversion efforts, Nanak dressed in a manner that illustrated his effort to integrate Hinduism and Islam. He wore a mango-colored jacket, over which he threw a white sheet (safa), and wore the special headdress of the Muslims and a necklace of bones. Then, in the manner of Hindus, he made a saffron mark on his forehead.

He carried his evangelistic activities far from home. Apparently he and his faithful companion turned to east and south India. At Puri, for example, he discussed various religious questions such as idols and their worship, the many and the One, matter and spirit. By speech and singing he sought to show the Brahmans the superiority of the rising Sikh religion.

Some say that Nanak also went as far as Ceylon. Another account has it that he took Mardana to Mecca, sacred shrine of Muslims, in Saudi Arabia. Garbed in the blue dress of Muslim pilgrims and with staff in hand, they carried ablution cups and prayer carpets for many months until they arrived at the sacred city. Here, according to the tradition, he disregarded Islamic custom. Instead of sleeping at night with his head toward the Kaaba, the sacred stone of Muslims, he turned his feet toward it. When asked why, he replied to the effect that his feet could not be turned in any direction in which God is not. From Mecca the two companions went on to Medina, another city sacred to Islam. There he did not hesitate to declare the truth as he saw it. He told the Muslims there that he rejected all sects and sought only to know the one God.

Upon their return to India, Mardana fell ill and died at Kartarpur. Nanak, sixty-nine years old, realized that his life also was drawing to a close. Upon reflection, he decided to appoint a successor who would continue to teach the faith. His wife insisted that he choose one of his sons. However, one was dissolute and the other lukewarm in his loyalty to his father; instead, Nanak selected Angad, a tried and devoted disciple. He gave Angad his blessing and withdrew to Kartarpur, a village on the Ravi River, to spend his remaining days in retirement. As he approached death, sitting in the open underneath an acacia tree, he fell into a trance. This was in October 1538 A.D.

According to tradition, Nanak's Muslim converts now declared that after his death they would bury him. The Sikhs who had been Hindus, however, said they would cremate him, according to their custom. Nanak, the great Guru, told the Hindus to put flowers on his right and the Muslims to put flowers on his left; he declared that those whose flowers were found fresh in the morning might have the disposal of his body. Some say his disciples sang as they pulled a sheet over him. He became still and died. When the sheet was removed the next morning, says the legend, there was nothing under it, and the flowers on both sides were in bloom. Even in the manner of his dying, Nanak had chosen neither Hinduism or Islam, but had initiated a new and different way.

HISTORY

A process of veneration set in after the death of Nanak. Sikhs began to believe that there were references to his life in Hindu and Islamic records. The prediction of his divinely appointed birth is included in the Sikh birth stories (*janamsakhis*). The miraculous

abounds; Nanak becomes an *avatar* or incarnation as in Hinduism
or a prophetic *mahdi* as in Islam. Stories about his remarkable activities during his ministry also arose. He was able to revive a dead
elephant and a dying man, cure and convert a leper, secure water
from dry ground, and freshen a withered fig tre, among other
miracles. Even his death, as we have seen, was conceived in terms of
miracle. Although he declared in his lifetime that his demerits could
not be numbered, that he uttered calumny day and night, and was
neither chaste, truthful, nor learned, he became in the eyes of his
followers—especially as the years went on—a divine savior. The
disciples thought of him as a deity, praying to him for pardon and
salvation. Nanak, who confirmed the transcendent nature of God in
his earthly teachings, became God himself in the eyes of his followers.

The history of Sikhism for two hundred years following its
founder's death was highly influenced by the ten Gurus who led
the movement during this period. The first was Angad, who received
his appointment directly from Nanak and necessarily faced the dis-
ruption caused by his death. Two tendencies were apparent at the
time. First, the newly-founded religion without its original leader
might be aborbed into either Hinduism or Islam. The possibility
was strong, for Sikhism appeared from certain viewpoints to be
merely a extension of either religion. Second, Angad faced the
chance that the new faith might fall apart. Without its strong
leader, it faced the prospect of decay.

Neither alternative came to pass. Angad was equal to the leadership of the new religion. By his considerable talents the gap between
birth and history was bridged.

He is noted for two other contributions. During Nanak's time
the Sikhs had provided a public kitchen in which disciples and their
friends could eat without regard for sex, caste, wealth, religion, or
any other distinction. Angad not only continued the ministry
of the public kitchen but enlarged it. This feature of Sikhism can
scarcely be considered the same type of social organization as the
sangha in Jainism and Buddhism. It was not an organized body of
believers; it was far more open, flexible, and limited in function.
But the public kitchen did provide an informal and regular meeting
place for faithful Sikhs.

Angad was also the leader in the formulation of a language by which Sikhism might be distinctively expressed. Building upon the vernacular of Nanak's time, he borrowed and invented an alphabet, with which he created Gurmukhi as the particular medium of Sikhism.

Angad (Guru from 1538 to 1552 A.D.) was followed by Guru Amar Das (1552-74 A.D.)—Nanak's son, Sri Chand, and others were passed over. Amar Das further strengthened Sikhism. Greatly interested in religious matters, he was a poet who employed verse as a means of extending the religion. He was an able administrator, giving wise and practical attention to the daily operations of the movement. Moreover, he had courage. Even in his time, the Sikhs maintained the Hindu custom of widow-burning (sati). Amar Das renounced the practice—in verse.

The question of the Guruship, however, was not completely settled. Datu, Angad's son, like Sri Chand before him had pressed his claim to office. In time Datu came to terms with Amar Das, but Sri Chand continued to claim the Guruship for himself. Since it was denied by the body of Sikhs, however, he became critical of the movement, saying that his father's religion was being perverted. He and his friends mourned what they considered the injustice of his not being the Guru and the lax interpretation that Sikhs allegedly gave to his father's teachings. As mourners, plunged into sorrow (udas), Sri Chand and his followers became advocates of asceticism. The sect became known as the Udasis.

Amar Das did not choose one of his own sons to succeed him; instead he named his daughter's husband, Jetha, who assumed the Guruship as Ram Das (1574-81), the fourth Guru. It was Ram Das who later introduced the principle of hereditary succession to the Guruship.

He was not an exceptional person. One of his main accomplishments was the establishment of Amritsar, thirty miles southeast of Lahore, as the central place of Sikh worship. Here, surrounded by Sikh disciples and a public kitchen, he established a settlement which was given the name of Ramdaspur, meaning the village of Ram Das.

The fifth Guru was Arjun (1581-1606). By the time of Arjun's leadership, Sikhism had become a fairly expansive religion. Its adherents were found in many villages throughout northwest India, led by assisting Gurus who expressed allegiance to Arjun. Arjun himself moved to Amritsar and there rebuilt the central shrine, giving it the title Har Mandir, or "everybody's temple." He built doorways on the four sides of the sign as a means of symbolizing the inclusiveness of Sikhism.

Arjun's notable accomplishment, however, was not that he rebuilt the shrine at Amritsar, nor that he gave up Nanak's distinctive dress, nor that he systematically collected taxes from the Sikhs. He also assembled the Adi Granth, the original scriptures of Sikhism. *Adi* means "original" and *Granth* means "book." Later, additions were made and the whole canon became known as the Granth Sahib, which means "Lord Book." The Adi Granth was placed in the center of the shrine at Amritsar as the most sacred symbol of Sikhism.

Later in life, Guru Arjun and other Sikhs apparently gave some encouragement to Khusraw, a Muslim youth who sought to over-throw his ruling father, Salim Jahangir. Khusraw, however, was promptly defeated and publicly humiliated before his father. Many Sikhs suffered as a consequence and Arjun was fined. Afterward, according to the tradition, he was tortured to death at Lahore and became the first martyr of the Sikhs. Today he is viewed as a deity —Guru Arjun Deva.

Har Gobind (1606-38) became the sixth Guru at the age of about ten years. Because of the military events of the closing days of Arjun's Guruship, Har Gobind was protected on his journeys by a bodyguard of sixty men and three hundred horsemen. Obviously the period in which the Muslim rulers of the Punjab were relatively unconcerned with the new religion had come to a close. It was necessary for Sikhs to be able to defend themselves, if necessary to go on the offensive. Har Gobind and his advisers appointed tax collectors so that they and the body of Sikhs might buy arms to protect themselves from attack. This Guru built a stronghold and took the sword, a religious emblem to all later Sikhs, as the badge of his leadership. Less passive than his predecessors, in the course of time he slew two rivals for his office.

Har Gobind was succeeded by his grandson, Har Rai (1638-60).

During this period Shah Jahan, one of the great and powerful Muslim emperors of India's history, died. His four sons, Dara, Shuja, Aurangzib, and Murad, fell into civil war over the succession. Har Rai unfortunately took sides with Dara, who, with his two other brothers, lost out in the struggle to Aurangzib. Har Rai was forced to send his son Ram Rai as a hostage to Aurangzib to bind his declaration of peaceful intentions. But peace was not secured, and Har Rai ended his career in defeat.

He was succeeded by another son, Har Kishan (1660-64), who was apparently approved as leader of the Sikhs by Aurangzib and spent a few years as Guru in an uneventful way. His leadership was cut short by a fatal attack of smallpox.

Teg Bahadur, a son of Har Gobind, became the ninth Guru (1664-75). Under his rule the peaceful religion of Nanak was further transformed into a military system. Indeed, the repressive measures of Aurangzib made strength in arms a virtue necessary to survival. Teg Bahadur left Amritsar and settled down in Anandpur, close to the Himalayas. This remote and well-protected location served him well in his defense for many years from the onslaughts of Aurangzib.

Teg Bahadur was moved by a missionary spirit. He organized ventures into other parts of India, even reaching Patna on the lower Ganges River. However, he was compelled to abandon these efforts by the pressure put on him and his followers by the forces of Aurangzib. One version of the events of the period recounts that the ninth Guru was made to report to the emperor in Delhi, a distance of about two hundred miles, under armed escort. There he was arrested as an unbeliever and public enemy and executed, his body put on display either beheaded or in pieces (the accounts differ). Another martyr graced the pages of Sikh history. Teg Hahadur was remembered for some of his writings which were included in later additions of the Granth Sahib.

The last Guru was Gobind Singh (1675-1708 A.D.). Because of unabated miiltary pressures this Guru continued to strengthen the Sikhs as a military force. At Dacca he established a stronghold which enabled him to withstand attack by the Muslim emperor. In the conduct of his office he was aided by Jita, his wife, who became an ideal for Sikh women of all time. She gave herself to community service and supported her husband with loyalty and intelligence.

Gobind Singh is noted in Sikh history for his establishment of a special order of Sikhs, called the Khalsa. These were an elite group who provided an instrument by which Sikh solidarity could be expressed and utter devotion to the cause galvanized in the carrying out of special obligations. These assumed at the time of initiation, included honoring the Gurus, as chewing tobacco and alcohol, and beginning to eat meat. Originally, according to tradition, Gobind Singh selected five of his most loyal followers. For them he poured water into an iron basin in which there was an Indian sweetmeat; the mixture was then stirred with a sword. Thereupon he gave five palmsful of the concoction to each of the five followers. He also sprinkled the mixture five times on each one's hair and eyes, after which the initiates or the baptized repeated: "The Pure are of God and the victory is to God." This declaration became the warcry of the Sikhs.

The followers were members of the Khalsa or the Pure. They became the lions (singhs) of Sikhism. Thereafter members of the Khalsa were distinguished by the use of the term "Singh" as a part of their names. Obviously, however, not all Sikhs in the past or today are Singh. Guru Gobind became a Singh by being himself baptized into the Khalsa by the first five members of the order, which was open to all who would satisfy its requirements. Its appeal was great, based as it was upon the dramatic ceremony of initiation, the warlike spirit it fostered—exemplified by the sword—and its attraction especially for lower-caste Hindus.

Gobind Singh also added to the Adi Granth by writing what is called the Granth of the Tenth Guru. His contributions were characteristic of himself and his times. He extolled the metal out of which swords were made as having a mysterious virtue. Some of his themes dealt in detail with his theory of warfare. But above all he continued Nanak's extreme emphasis upon the importance of the Name and its repetition by the faithful.

With Aurangzib's death in 1707, Gobind Singh had a temporary respite from military activities. Two sons of the Muslim emperor fought for the throne in the north while a third stood ready in the south. Some reports say that Gobind Singh joined forces with the successful son (the one in the south) and was murdered two or three months later. Other accounts give other versions of his death. At any rate, he instructed his followers that no more Gurus were to be appointed. He told them that they should consider the Granth Sahib their Guru. Thus ended the succession of ten Gurus from Nanak to Gobind Singh.

The Sikhs continued, however, to engage in warfare. By the time the British came to India they had succeeded in controlling the whole of the Punjab. In 1849, Maharaja Dhulip Singh, the last Sikh ruler of the Punjab, surrendered to the British. As a sign of his loyalty and that of his followers he sent the famed Kohinoor diamond to Queen Victoria. From that time on the Sikhs were safely on the side of the British. Even when the Indian Mutiny broke out in 1857, the Sikhs, especially the Singhs of the Khalsa, supported the British. For this they were rewarded by being made adjuncts to British police and military power in several parts of Asia.

Today, however, the bulk of the Sikhs are not active warriors, but peaceful agriculturalists and traders in the Punjab. During the partition of colonial India, many returned to the use of force against both Muslims and Hindus. Their home territory, the Punjab, was divided between Pakistan and India. More recently they have called for a separate Sikh state. By the end of 1965 this demand was granted.

SCRIPTURES

The final form of the sacred scriptures of Sikhism is called the Granth Sahib or "Lord Book." This consists of a large collection of short and long poems devoted to extolling of the name of God and to the implications of Sikhism for practical living. The scriptures were composed by several dozen authors who inevitably expressed their individual sentiments. Several of the writers have only slight relationship to Sikhism: Kabir and Ramananda, who were primarily

Hindu reformers and lived prior to Nanak, are contributors. Also, several Hindu and Islamic saints (*bhagats*) have contributed to the Granth Sahib.

These scriptures are noteworthy because of being written in at least six languages in addition to several dialects: Gurmukhi, Multani, Persian, Prakrit, Hindi, and Marathi. Such diversity in language makes it difficult for the Sikhs, both the untrained and the scholarly, to read and study the scriptures in their entirety. Probably there are very few people in the world capable of reading the whole canon. The Granth Sahib, however, is not used by loyal Sikhs in the same manner as Christians and Jews, for example, use their own sacred scriptures. Practically no Sikhs are familiar with the Granth Sahib, since the scriptures do not play an educational role in nurturing the religious life of the Sikhs. No extensive development of biblical studies exists in Sikhism as compared to Judaism and Christianity.

An added deterrent to the widespread use of the Granth Sahib is the fact that there is no separation of words in the original languages. This practice, of course, follows Sanskrit, in which the words also are not separated. But in the several languages in which the Granth Sahib is written, no line of separation between words has developed because the early interpreters (*gyanis*) considered it profane to separate the words of the sacred writings.

The compilation of the Adi Granth or the original book was the work of Arjun, the fifth Guru. Into it he put Nanak's Japji, the religious poetry that Gurus Amar Das and Ram Das had composed, and the verses of Kabir and other Hindu saints. Arjun was faced with the task of selecting materials from his own time and the past that were suitable to creation of a holy book. Obviously he made choices not only to include but to exclude.

Sikhism also possesses noncanonical writings which date from its earliest days. Arjun contributed his own materials, such as the lengthy "Peace-Jewel" (*sukhmani*) and the long acrostic, the Fifty-two (*bawan akhari*). His contributions are not noted for their philosophic profundity, but stress the importance of the Name and are cast in meditational form.

Generally the Sikhs prefer an arrangement of their sacred scriptures which does not stress the individual authorship of its parts. But in the main the contributions of the first, second, third, fourth, fifth, and ninth Gurus are placed at the beginning. Actually it is difficult to distinguish the contributions of the several Gurus because all used the name Nanak as their *nom-de-plume* (*takhallus*). Yet Nanak clearly wrote some part of the Granth Sahib. In this respect he is distinctive. The other founders of religions originating in India, Mahavira and the Buddha, so far as is known did not write any part of the sacred scriptures of their faiths.

Although the Granth Sahib is neglected by the Sikhs and its details practically unknown to them, it is highly revered. At the chief shrine of Sikhism at Amritsar there are no images, for Sikhism is devoted to the one God. But the Granth Sahib is there in a central place. It is treated as though it were God. It is dressed every morning in rich brocade and placed on a low throne under a jeweled canopy. Every night it is placed in a golden bed within a sacred chamber. Relays of temple priests publicly read the Granth Sahib day by day through its entirety.

TEACHINGS

Sikhism is a syncretic religion. It originated no new teachings, but relied mainly upon Hinduism and Islam for its doctrines. Yet Sikhism is itself, that is, it is an independent religion. It did not merely take in undigested chunks of Hinduism and Islam. This is made clear, for example, in the composition of the Granth Sahib. Nanak and his successors could have surveyed the vast literature of Hinduism and Islam, taking intact whatever sections most accurately reflected their teachings. But this was not done. A new sacred scripture was created. This embodies ideas taken from Hinduism and Islam, but reflects them in its own way. The Granth Sahib very clearly rejects parts of the scriptures and teachings of Hinduism and Islam.

In its teachings Sikhism both agrees and disagrees with its parent religions. It agrees with one strand of Hinduism in its stress upon a transcendent and virtually unknowable deity. In Hinduism this deity is Brahma. Sikhism reveres a single deity, for which it has various designations. It accepted, moreover, the Hindu teachings on *karma* and rebirth.

On the other hand, Sikhism disagrees with a number of Hindu teachings; it renounced Hindu polytheism, pilgrimages, ritualism, and asceticism. It teaches that all of these stand in the way of the practice of the true worship of the Formless One. Similarly idolatry is outlawed in Sikhism. The new religion also renounced the Hindu caste system, teaching that at least all Sikhs are equal. Women are given a higher social position in Sikhism than in Hinduism, but are not accorded full equality. Sikhism also permits the eating of meat.

It is in agreement with a number of Islamic teachings, of which the chief is the emphasis upon the Wholly Other. Sikhism, like Islam, teaches the absolute supremacy of God. Salvation is secured through submission (*islam*) to God, loyalty to the founder of the religion as a divine prophet, and the repetition of prescribed prayers and the Name of the Nameless. Sikhism also agrees on the importance of a series of leaders or prophets who have succeeded the original founder of the religion. Like Islam, it developed a militaristic church-state for which a central shrine, Amritsar, (like Mecca) is important. It also strongly opposes idolatry and similar practices.

Sikhism disagrees with Islam, however, in several ways. Both its founder and its deity are more humane. Fasting as in Islam's month of Ramadan is not viewed as a religious requirement, and the goal of life as entrance into a pleasurable paradise is not stressed. The sacred scriptures of Sikhism are the product of many persons rather than one.

Like all other complex religions, Sikhism has been unable to keep its followers united. Over the years it has been riven by sectarianism. Some of the minor groups are: Handalis, the Ramraiyas, the Mine of Pirthi Chand, the Dhirmaliye, and the Masandis. Major groups include the Nanakpanthis, the Udasis, the Akalis or Nihangs or Shahidis, the Nirmalis, and the Sewapanthis. The latter five sects will bear brief mention.

First, the Nanakpanthis came to be followers of the path (*panthis*) of Guru Nanak. Although the majority do not claim to be blood-descendants of the Guru, some do claim to be so related. The Nanakpanthis consider themselves the oldest and most orthodox of Sikh sects.

Second, the Udasis, already mentioned, were founded by Nanak's son Sri Chand. They are obviously among the oldest of the sects, dating even to the time of Nanak. Today they operate as a clearly independent and strong group with an elective Guruship. They stress what they assert was Nanak's sense of estrangement from the world. A keynote of their teaching is sorrow (*udas*), a state of sadness at the sinfulness of the world. Amar Das, the third Guru, specifically repudiated the Udasis as Sikhs. The formation of the Khalsa, moreover, which was committed to Sikhs living fully in the world, further separated the Udasis from the mainstream of Sikhism. Lacking political ambition, they have not favored the expression of Sikhism in a church-state and have tended to be quietistic and withdrawn from the principal secular involvements of other Sikhs. Sometimes they even become monks, distinguished by shaven heads and a renunciation of family and other social relationships.

Third, the Akalis or Ninhangs or Shahidis comprise another major sectarian group. Their names connote immortals (*akalis*), reckless ones (*nihangs*), or martyrs or witnesses (*shahidis*). The Akalis believed that God's true name is the Timeless (*akal*). They held that there is no necessity to be either only ascetics or militarists; to them both functions were obligatory upon Sikhs. In the ordinary course of daily life the Akalis were distrustful of the attractions of the world and lived ascetically. But they were quite willing to be reckless witnesses to their faith. They antedate the creation of the Khalsa and became its most vehement and sacrificial advocates. Wearing a distinctive blue uniform and accustomed to fighting with great skill either singly or in groups, they were often feared both within and outside of Sikhism.

Fourth, the Nirmalis came into existence during the Guruship of Gobind Singh. Their name means "those witout blemish." At first they wore white clothes and remained active in the general movements of Sikhism, but later they began wearing ochre-colored clothes and maintained a separate order under a leader and a council of their own. The Nirmalis did not marry and generally led ascetic lives. They tolerantly went on pilgrimage to Hindu shrines, although they opposed the caste system and begging as exemplified in Hinduism.

Fifth, the Sewapanthis, or those of the "service-way," laid primary stress upon impartial service. According to tradition, Kanhaiya, a water-carrier and founder of the sect, during the Mughal siege of Anandpur gave nonmilitary service to both sides. Gobind Singh rebuked him, but Kanhaiya reminded the Guru that service in itself was meritorious according to Gobind Singh's teachings, whereupon the Guru gave him his blessing. Sikhs grouped themselves about Kanhaiya and with him engaged in various forms of service. The Sewapanthis refuse all rewards.

The Khalsa Sikhs, mentioned earlier, also comprise a notable group within Sikhism.

Historically these various sects, parties, bands, and groups within Sikhism have been called *misls* or equals. In fact they have never been equal, and they always maintain some kind of individual autonomy. Yet under certain circumstances, such as a common enemy, they have succeeded in coming together into a loose confederation.

God

Sikhism is strongly monotheistic. In this respect it is much more in agreement with Islam than with Hinduism. Islam taught that God is One and far transcends any and all deities advocated by other religions. Sikhism follows Islam faithfully on this score. It is true that monotheistic teachings are found within Hinduism. The Upanishads, for example, impatient with the Vedic pantheon, actively advocate Brahma as the god above all gods. But Hinduism, not only in the Vedic period but later, has been amenable to other teachings about God. In Nanak's time it was largely characterized by polytheism; it is against this expression of Hinduism that Nanak revolted, and on this basis he rejected the authority of the Vedas. He could not agree that there are many gods and that the individual or group should have the privilege of selecting the one or ones that particularly suit his fancy. Nanak and later Sikhism emphasized the importance of the singleness of God and of this reality beside every other imagined deity.

Sikhism designates the deity as the True Name (*Sat Nam*). This designation begins the Adi Granth and each hymn in the sacred scriptures, as well as appearing frequently throughout the Granth Sahib. But other names for the True Name are also found in the Granth Sahib. For example, it makes use of Islamic names like Allah and Khudda (the Glorious). The names of such Hindu deities as Brahma, Param Brahma, Hari, Parameshvar, and Rama appear, as well as others which are not strictly to be found in either Hinduism or Islam. Thus Sikhism, while believing that the True Name designates the God above all gods, is not reluctant to use the names of the deities of other religions. It establishes one caution, however: namely, that no one confuse the name of a lesser deity with the name or being of the True Name.

Nanak was never tired of preaching the glory and the greatness of God. He thought that the True Name is self-created and self-existent, that he pervades everything in the whole creation and is responsible for the conduct of the greatest and smallest affairs. Nobody knows the limits of God; only God himself knows how great he is. All descriptions of the greatness of God and all praise of him fall far short of his reality. The power of the True Name was most apparent to Nanak, who believed that this can free the believer from the control of *karma* and the necessity for rebirth.

Yet God is not only absolute (*nirdun*); he is also personal (*satun*). He is a personal Being who is capable of being loved and honored. Although he has fashioned the worlds of existence and supports them by his power, he is also concerned personally with his creatures. The True Name has not undergone an incarnation, although his presence may be found in those persons and events which others claim to be an expression of the divine. All men are inscribed with his name and his moral presence. He does not belong to any particular people, whether Hindu or Muslim, but is the universal dispenser of life. Thus God is one, absolute, eternal, transcendent, immanent, omnipresent, and real.

Sikhism never developed its teachings in such detail or as profoundly as did Hinduism, Jainism, and Buddhism. Therefore, it is difficult to say how the religion conceives the composition of the self, society, and nature. This faith does teach that the world is of second importance to God. Everything, according to the Granth Sahib, is thoroughly false; the whole world is passing away. Since the world is transitory and an illusion, men should put their trust in the True Name. Apparently Nanak accepted a form of the Hindu doctrine of *maya* or illusion. He taught that the self, society, and nature possess only a derived and tentative reality. They have no worth in themselves, are essentially unreal.

Nanak also taught his disciples (*shikshas*) that they were bound by the law of *karma*. This law, bringing to each person both now and forever the consequences of his actions, binds the individual by a force or fate which is not given to individual human beings ultimately to control, except through the power of the Name. Believers are liable to the process of rebirth. Yet a state like *nirvana* can be attained by those upon whom God looks favorably and who endlessly repeat his Name. Individuality is eternally obliterated by being fully absorbed in God.

The Person

Sikhism teaches that man may find salvation by knowing God or by being ultimately absorbed into God. This doctrine is appropriate to the emphasis in Sikhism upon the wholly-otherness of deity. Man is helpless; God is all-powerful. Salvation is not fundamentally achieved by any action open to the believer. He can think upon and repeat the name of God endlessly. He can go on pilgrimages, worship in shrines, and use all kinds of religious practices, but these alone will not suffice. Sikhism teaches that man's salvation depends upon the grace of God: the unmerited beneficence of the True Name. God chooses to redeem men, despite their own action or lack of it. This teaching of the grace of God is found preeminently in Islam, but the Upanishads also teach that the spiritual regeneration of man is initially dependent upon divine pleasure.

In practice, the seeming paradox between the transcendence and the grace of God is resolved in Sikhism by its emphasis upon the importance of the superior wisdom of the Guru. Sikhism requires that every believer be a disciple (*shiksha*) of a Guru. The believer must surrender himself totally to the Guru—a sign of his total submissiveness to the True Name. The Guru has the responsibility of instructing the believer in the true faith by which the grace of God may become operative for him. Similarly, in the moral life Sikhism lays stress not on rules or laws, but upon discipleship. The Guru is a model for the disciple in his daily conduct. The goal of the disciple is to achieve that higher quality of life which is exemplified in living Gurus, and more particularly those virtues which were taught and lived by the first ten Gurus in Sikhism's history. The concept of the Guru provides a basis for a high degree of individualism within Sikhism.

But Sikhism does control behavior in specific ways. The new order of life initiated with the Khalsa requires that Sikhs of that persuasion obligate themselves to what is called the five K's (*kukkas*). First, they should wear their hair long on their heads and chins (*kes*). Second, they should wear a comb in the hair on their heads (*kangha*). Third, they should wear short drawers next to their skin (*kachk*). Fourth, they should wear an iron or steel bracelet (*kara*). Fifth, they should always wear a two-edged dagger (*khanda*) in the street. Sikhs are also required to comb their hair at least twice a day and to bathe often. In the Khalsa they are encouraged to abstain from all stimulants, including alcoholic beverages. Tobacco is also denied. In contrast to the vegetarianism of Hinduism, however, the Sikhs of the Khalsa are encouraged to eat meat, although not pork. By this teaching, Sikhism is supposed by some of its interpreters to have placed man on a higher order of divine creation than the lower animals. Earlier Sikhs were critical of prohibitions against meat-eating because they put all living things on a basis of equality.

Of course, these prescriptions for conduct have not been maintained perfectly by all Sikhs. Later interpreters of the Adi Granth, for example, have found a statement which to them justifies the use of spiritous liquors.

Another formulation of the Sikh code of conduct lists three general injunctions. First, the Sikh should always speak the truth and never tell lies. Second, he should beware of even an unconscious sin. Third, he should not "step on the bed of another's wife" even in a dream.

Sikhism's teaching on the afterlife has much more in common with Hinduism, with its emphasis on *karma* and rebirth, than with Islam, which teaches a belief in judgment, paradise, and hell. According to Islam Allah one day will judge his creatures. On this doomsday, rewards and punishments will be distributed. Unbelievers will go to hell, a place where they will broil in encompassing sheets of fire. The righteous, however, will enter paradise, a place filled with tempting food, agreeable rest, flowing rivers, and sensuous pleasures. Sikhism rejected this view of the afterlife. It does not teach a decisive judgment day nor a joyous paradise. The human being, according to Sikhism, is bound by *karma* and rebirth. He can escape these only by being absorbed into God. This absorption connotes mystical union and comes about by the grace of God and the faithful repetition of the True Name.

Society

Among the living religions of the world are three fundamental attitudes toward the world. First, some are world-accepting. The Vedic literature, for example, fits this category. In this view, not all the world is good by any means, but fundamentally and especially the goodness of the world is evident through religious exercises. Second, some are world-rejecting. Non-Vedic parts of Hinduism, Jainism, and Buddhism to a large degree express this view. The world from this standpoint is a thoroughly evil place or condition, and man is fundamentally incapable of genuine goodness in it. He is called upon to escape it by one means or another and find his fulfillment in a different sphere of reality. Third, some have mixed views regarding the world. Thus in Zoroastrianism the world is conceived as a battleground in which the forces of good and evil are relatively equal. Judaism, Christianity, and Islam also express this view.

Sikhism possesses both world-accepting and world-rejecting tendencies. Groups within it have been willing and even eager to

enter fully into the world's affairs. The soldierly strain in Sikhism
is evidence of a belief in the possibility of man's successful management of his social relations, even if force must be his instrument.
Sikhism also broke with Hinduism's vegetarianism and acknowledged
priorities among living things.

On the other hand, the Sikhs have world-rejecting tendencies.
Several of its sects have engaged in ascetic disciplines, though Nanak
himself was distrustful of such religious practices as idolatry, pilgrimages, fasting, and sacrifices. Aside from its existence as a church-
state, Sikhism has never developed an organized program of social
amelioration. The Granth Sahib is confined largely to teachings
about the Glorious One and the relationship of the individual
believer in his daily action to the True Name.

This faith did, however, repudiate the caste system. Nanak taught
that all human beings are to be regarded as brothers. In his initial
declaration after his divine call and commission, he declared
that God had introduced a new dispensation in which there was no
Hindu and no Muslim. The early movement took converts from both
Hinduism and Islam, and social barriers were abandoned in the
public kitchens, places where the faithful ate together. These
kitchens, a feature of early Sikhism in which an order very roughly
similar to the *sangha* in Jainism and Buddhism was created, violated
one of the strong prohibitions in the Hindu teaching on caste. And
although the caste system was repudiated by Nanak and his followers
the fact of caste persisted and affected, for example, intermarriage
among Hindu converts.

Sikhism taught a higher regard for women than did Hinduism.
According to tradition, Nanak questioned the inferiority of women,
saying that they gave birth to the greatest men. Women are the
equal of men in that they are held equally responsible for their
actions to God. God showers his grace upon men and women indis-
criminately. Sikhism early condemned the Hindu practice of widow-
burning (*sati*).

Respect for women is also shown by the prohibition of early
marriage. This Hindu practice was repudiated by the Sikhs, who
taught that marriage (*shadi*) should take place at maturity. The

ceremony itself should be preceded by an engagement celebration in which the girl's parents invite the relatives of the boy, but not the boy himself, to a ceremony in the home. In the ceremony a copy of the Adi Granth is presented, some sweetmeats shared, and plans made for the wedding. Sikhs are encouraged to marry only other Sikhs and divorce can be secured only if a man or woman is unchaste. Adultery is looked upon with strong disfavor.

The Sikhs have yet to develop their own distinctive social institutions in adequate forms and numbers. Education, for example, is relatively scarce among them. They make use of the Guru, but have failed to develop an authentic educational system. Recently, however, some Sikhs have come to recognize the importance of formal education and have developed some schools of their own, including one college in Amritsar and another in Bombay. Since they are primarily agriculturists, they may find that the development of an adequate educational system will tend to open new vocational vistas. These may have far-reaching consequences for the main body of Sikhs.

Sikhism, which began as an effort to combine and supersede two great faiths, became in the course of time an independent religion. Hinduism and Islam were not replaced. Today the three faiths exist side by side, along with the other religions, in both Pakistan and India—that regional seedbed which has provided more flowers of religion for its own people and for the world than any other land.

ANNOTATED BIBLIOGRAPHY ON SIKHISM

1 ARCHER, JOHN. *The Sikhs: A Study in Comparative Religion.* Princeton, N. J.: Princeton University Press, 1946. A history of the Sikhs and an analysis of their teachings and relations with other groups in India.

2 BANERJEE, INDUBHUSAN. *Evolution of the Khalsa: The Foundation of the Sikh Panth*, Vol. I. Calcutta: University of Calcutta, 1936. The history of Sikhism to 1604, by which time the *Granth Sahib* was completed.

3 CUNNINGHAM, JOSEPH. *A History of the Sikhs.* New York: Oxford University Press, 1918. A history from the origin of Sikhism to the Battles of the Sutlej.

4 FIELD, DOROTHY. *The Religion of the Sikhs.* New York: E. P. Dutton & Co., 1914. Information on the Sikhs, with selections from their scriptures.

5 MACAULIFFE, M. A. *The Sikh Religion: Its Gurus, Sacred Writings, and Anthems.* Oxford: Clarendon Press, 1909. Translations of the *Granth Sahib* interspersed in the lives of the Gurus of Sikhism.

6 MACAULIFFE, M. A., et. al. *The Sikh Religion: A Symposium.* Calcutta: Susil Gupta Private, 1958. A collection of papers by specialists on various aspects of the religion of the Sikhs.

7 RAM, SARDHA. *History of the Sikhs.* Calcutta: Susil Gupta Private, Ltd., 1959. A rich source on the history of the Sikhs.

8 *Selections from the Sacred Writings of the Sikhs,* by various translators. New York: The Macmillan Co., 1960. A good introduction to the scriptures of Sikhism.

9 SINGH, KRUSHWANT. *A History of the Sikhs*, 2 vols. Princeton, N. J.: Princeton University Press, 1963, 1966. An indispensable source for the history of the Sikhs.

10 SINGH, TEJA. *Sikhism: Its Ideals and Institutions.* New York: Longmans, Green & Co., 1938. A compendium of Sikh doctrine bearing on the questions of God and man, the way of salvation, and other topics.

11 TRUMPP, ERNEST, translator. *The Adi Granth or Holy Scriptures of the Sikhs*. London: Trubner, 1877. The early part of the *Granth Sahib* in English.

ANNOTATED BIBLIOGRAPHY
ON THE WORLD'S LIVING RELIGIONS

*1   ALLEN, E. L. *Christianity Among the Religions*. Boston: Beacon Press, 1960. Discusses the relations of Christianity with the other religions.

2   BACH, MARCUS. *Major Religions of the World*. New York: Abingdon Press, 1959. Covers a number of the living religions in the simplest manner.

*3   BERRY, GERALD. *Religions of the World*. New York: Barnes & Noble, 1956. A brief and general summary.

*4   BOUQUET, ALAN. *Sacred Books of the World*. Baltimore: Penguin Books, 1954. An anthology.

5   BRADEN, CHARLES S. *The Scriptures of Mankind: An Introduction*. New York: The Macmillan Co., 1952. A study, including quotations from the great bibles of the world.

*6   ———. *The World's Religions: A Short History*. New York: Apex Books, Abingdon Press, 1954. A concise account of the great religions of today.

7   BURTT, EDWIN. *Man Seeks the Divine: A Study in the History and Comparison of Religion*. New York: Harper & Brothers, 1957. A sympathetic exposition of how man's faith has been expressed through the ages.

*8   CHAMPION, SELWYN GURNEY, and SHORT, DOROTHY, eds. *Readings from World Religions*. Greenwich, Conn.: Premier Books, Fawcett Publications, 1959. Contains selections from the scriptures of the four religions of India.

*9   GAER, JOSEPH. *The Wisdom of the Living Religions*. New York: Dodd, Mead, New York, 1956. The teachings of the living religions presented through their sayings, maxims, and parables.

*10   ———. *How the Great Religions Began*, rev. ed. New York: Signet Key Books, New American Library, 1958. Discusses the

* Paperback.

world's living religions in an elementary fashion, but is very weak on Hinduism.

11 HUME, ROBERT. *The World's Living Religions: An Historical Sketch,* rev. by Charles S. Braden. New York: Charles Scribner's Sons, 1959. A highly factual summary of eleven living religions.

12 JAMES, EDWARD. *History of Religions.* New York: Harper & Brothers, 1957. A responsible presentation of the essentials of the subject.

13 KITAGAWA, JOSEPH. *Religions of the East.* Philadelphia: Westminster Press, 1960. Primarily a description of the holy communities in Confucianism and other Chinese religions, and in Hinduism, Buddhism, and Islam.

14 KONOW, STEN and TUXEN, POUL. *The Religions of India.* Copenhagen: G. E. C. Gad, 1949. An introduction which mainly stresses Hinduism and omits Sikhism.

*15 LANDIS, BENSON. *World Religions.* New York: Everyman Paperbacks, E. P. Dutton & Co., 1960. A brief guide to the principal teachings of the world's chief religious systems.

16 NIELSEN, NIELS C., JR. *A Layman Looks at World Religions.* St. Louis, Mo.: Bethany Press, 1962. A brief and introductory book.

17 NOSS, JOHN. *Man's Religions,* New York: The Macmillan Co., 1949. An excellent, although long, textbook.

18 PARRINDER, E. GEOFFREY. *Worship in the World's Religions.* New York: Association Press, 1961. The practice and devotions of the followers of the world's living religions are described.

*19 POTTER, CHARLES FRANCIS. *The Great Religious Leaders.* New York: Washington Square Press, 1962. Contains the biographies, among others, of Buddha and Nanak.

*20 ROSS, FLOYD, and HILLS, TYNETTE. *The Great Religions by Which Men Live.* Greenwich, Conn.: Premier Books, Fawcett Publications, 1961. Employs a review of several of the living religions to supply answers to personal questions.

*21 SMITH, HUSTON. *The Religions of Man.* New York Mentor Books, New American Library, 1958. The basic teachings of the major faiths.

22 SPIEGELBERG, FREDERIC. *Living Religions of the World.* Englewood Cliffs, N. J.: Prentice-Hall, 1956. A college textbook.

NAME INDEX

SUBJECT INDEX

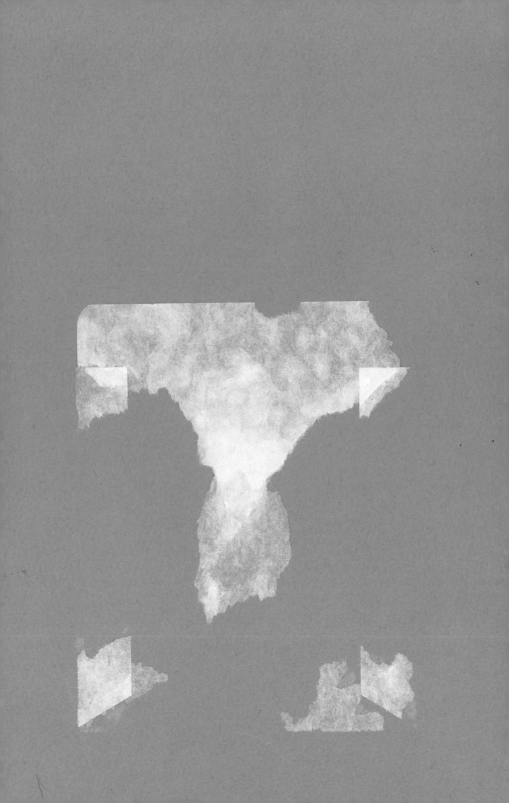